D0005119

The Visual Slide Revolution

Transforming overloaded text slides
into persuasive presentations

Dave Paradi

Copyright © 2008 by Dave Paradi

All rights reserved.

Published in Canada and the United States
by Communications Skills Press.

Library and Archives Canada Cataloguing in Publication

Paradi, Dave, 1966-
 The visual slide revolution : five steps to transform overloaded text
slides into persuasive presentations / Dave Paradi.

ISBN 978-0-9698751-8-5

 1. Microsoft PowerPoint (Computer file). 2. Presentation graphics
software.
I. Title.

T385.P3675 2008   005.5'8   C2008-902056-1

Printed in Canada and the United States of America

www.VisualSlideRevolution.com

Cover design by Dotti Albertine
Cover photo by Dave Paradi
Editing services by David Yanor

PowerPoint® is a registered trademark of Microsoft Corporation.

CONTENTS

Why are presentations to decision-makers so poor? Why persuasive visuals? The research supporting the use of visuals. Understanding Persuasion. Conclusion: Persuasive Visuals Work.

What is a visual slide? What is the KWICK Method? The KWICK Method. Slide Makeover Examples.

The Data Analysis Process. Writing the Slide Headline. Slide Makeover Examples.

Words & Phrases that suggest a visual. Slide Makeover Examples.

The Visual Slide Revolution

Transforming overloaded text slides
into persuasive presentations

Acknowledgments

A book like this could not have been written without the hard work and contributions of many. I am indebted to all the audiences and clients who have helped push my thinking in these areas. It is only through the challenge that we become better.

I also want to acknowledge my colleagues in the speaking and presentation industries who have inspired me to write and recognized my expertise in the effectiveness of presentation visuals.

Finally, my family's sacrifices must be acknowledged. They selflessly gave me the time and space to imagine, plan, write, review and rewrite. My wife, Sheila, and our children, Andrew and Laura, have been very supportive throughout this effort and for that I will always be grateful.

INTRODUCTION

The Visual Slide Revolution

Presentations, especially those employing computer-generated visuals, have become the standard communication tool for businesses and governments today. But most presentations that are designed and delivered are not as effective as they could be. They are usually a series of overloaded text slides read word-for-word by the presenter. Presenters who want to be successful have to join the Visual Slide Revolution to stand head and shoulders above the normal boring, text-filled presentations.

Organizations have trained their staff on presentations skills and have sent them on technical training courses to learn all the features of the software used to create the visuals, but neither activity addresses the core problem. What is missing is the training on how to effectively use visuals to persuade an audience of decision-makers to act on your message. The information in this book fills that gap.

Chapter one explains why so many presentations fail to achieve their goals. It also relays what presenters need to know about the fundamentals of persuasion. This information sets the stage for the introduction in chapter two of the KWICK method of creating and delivering persuasive presentation visuals. These five steps are then described in detail in chapters three to seven. Once you understand the steps, chapter eight gives concrete suggestions on how to start using the KWICK method in your next presentation. The Appendix lists additional resources to use as you develop your skills and deliver effective visual presentations.

The information in this book is not specific to any presentation software product (PowerPoint, Keynote, etc.), but applies to any presentation software you may use. Since you probably already know how to use that software (or can easily learn by acquiring a book that shows you how), this book does not contain technical "how to" instructions for any of the software packages. The focus of this book is on structure, design and delivery of presentations that effectively use visuals.

CHAPTER ONE

Why Do You Need Persuasive Visuals?

Why are presentations to decision-makers so poor?

Most presentations to decision-makers are done by specialists or analysts. It is appropriate to mention that the term "decision-maker" denotes anyone who might use presentation material to make or influence a decision, no matter their level in an organization.

Let us assume the staff person has been asked to present to one or more decision-makers on a specific topic. It is a plum opportunity for the staff person to gain visibility at a high level in the organization. But what happens? Almost every time, the specialist ends up spewing endless reams of data at the audience, usually in slides filled with text and numbers. The end result is that decision-makers are more confused than before. Decisions get delayed or made on incomplete or incorrect assumptions.

Why does this happen? Analysts and specialists focus on the detailed data in their work because it is their job to do so. They may be responsible for analyzing market data, operational data, financial data, competitor data, economic data or other data that is relevant to their business. They are immersed in it every day. When given the opportunity to present it to decision-makers, they mistakenly believe that the audience wants to see all the data that they deal with every day. The specialist feels that since the data is so important, the audience will surely not want to miss any of it.

Unfortunately, this viewpoint is wrong. This is related to what the Heath brothers call "The Curse of Knowledge," which we will discuss in a later section.

What many specialists and analysts fail to recognize is that there is a difference between data and information. Data are raw numbers that reflect reality in a market or business. The job of the specialist is to take the data, analyze it and create conclusions that non-experts can easily understand.

Those conclusions are called information. Presenting information allows decision-makers to weigh the importance of what has been presented and take the appropriate action. By presenting the information visually, it is that much easier to understand, discuss and use in decision-making.

The specialist must adjust his/her mindset. The audience does not need to be fed all the raw background data that went into an analysis. Instead, the specialist needs to understand that the decision-maker needs to answer the critical question: What conclusion do I need to know that will impact my decision-making?

Once specialists adopt this viewpoint, their focus will change and their presentations will improve dramatically.

Why persuasive visuals?

It helps to look at how we have effectively communicated in the past. Thousands of years ago, we drew on a cave wall. The crude drawings told a story to all observers. Formal language was not yet in use, but traditions, history and important lessons were still effectively passed on. Each of us can also remember how important stories and traditions are passed on in our own families. Many of us can recall sitting with a grandparent, uncle or aunt and having them show us an old photo or yellowed newspaper clipping, telling us the tale of that day or event. So we know about visuals on a personal level and how visuals have been a powerful means of storytelling and communicating ideas for thousands of years.

We can look at creating a message that gets acted upon as a two-step process. First, we need to determine the right points to focus on and the proper order in which to deliver them. This is where the principles of persuasion can guide us. They show us what ideas and approaches persuade most effectively. Later in this chapter we will examine the six principles of persuasion and how to apply them to our business presentations.

Once we know what points we want to make, the next step is to create effective ways of making those points stick in the mind of the audience member. Here is where "sticky" ideas help. The characteristics of those ideas are reviewed later in this chapter. These qualities inform the design of our visuals and how we deliver them.

Most of the rest of this book is devoted to creating persuasive visuals that contain the right message in the right order delivered in an effective way.

Why use visuals instead of text? Because research has demonstrated overwhelmingly that visuals are more effective.

The research supporting the use of visuals

The first piece of evidence supporting the use of visuals over text comes from a survey of audience members. They were asked what annoyed them about the poor PowerPoint presentations they were used to seeing. Please note that

PowerPoint here is used as a proxy for any presentation that uses visuals to help convey the message.

The top three annoyances were:

- Speaker read the slides to the audience—67.4%
- Full sentences instead of bullet points—45.4%
- Text so small it could not be read—45.0%

(The survey was conducted online in September/October 2007. Respondents were asked to select the top three annoyances out of a list of ten.)

The most extreme example cited in the surveys concerned a presentation at a conference, most likely an academic conference. The presenter reviewed a paper that had been published in a journal. He prepared for his talk by scanning each page of the journal article on to a slide. He then proceeded to stand up and read the entire article, word-for-word to the audience. Just imagine how boring that would have been.

The clear conclusion from the survey results is that by using primarily text slides, you have a high likelihood of annoying your audience instead of informing them. Audiences will be patient for a few minutes, but if you have lost them in a sea of text, you may never regain either their goodwill or their attention. Text-only slides that contain a transcript of what the speaker is saying are to be avoided at all cost.

The second piece of research derives from Professor Richard E. Mayer's book, "Multimedia Learning." Dr. Mayer is one of the most published and respected academics on the most effective use of media when presenting ideas. His research has been widely published in numerous journals and is referenced often by others.

We can apply his principles of media design to the creation of persuasive visuals. His principles most relevant to our discussion are as follows:

Multimedia Principle: Audience members understand better when both words and corresponding pictures are used rather than words alone. When we speak of pictures, we include other types of visual representations as well.

Modality & Redundancy Principles: Audiences understand better when our words are spoken rather than displayed as text for them (and us) to read.

Professor Mayer's research strongly suggests we should design presentation slides that we can speak to, instead of read. This echoes the results from the "annoying presentation" survey. Ideally, these slides should contain pictures and other types of visual representations of our information.

The final research comes from Professor Allan Paivio. His Dual-Coding Theory of Cognition states that information is processed in two distinct channels in the human brain: one deals with visual information and one handles verbal information. The brain codes each type of information differently and we comprehend best when the visual and verbal information is consistent with each other. If there are multiple or conflicting inputs in a single channel, it leads to difficulty in interpreting the different inputs, since they compete with each other in the single channel.

When we apply Professor Paivio's theory to business presentations, we recognize that a well-designed, clear visual that is explained verbally will result in the best understanding by the audience. Confusing visuals or reading text that is displayed will cause overload in one of the channels and leads to poorer results for our presentation. Again, Professor Paivio's work supports the idea that visuals, properly used in presentation, lead to more successful outcomes from our presentations.

The case for using visuals is irrefutable. It is based on research that has been consistently proven in academic circles. If we are to design visuals that persuade others to action, we next need to understand the principles of persuasion.

Understanding Persuasion

The appropriate place to begin a discussion of persuasion is with the classic book on the psychology of persuasion, "Influence," by Professor Robert B. Cialdini. In his book, Professor Cialdini outlines the six universal principles of persuasion that explain why people say "yes." What follows is an explanation of his principles and their application to business presentations.

Principle of Reciprocation: We should try to repay, in kind, what another person has provided us.

Application for business presentations: The common application of this principle is that when we give something to another, we expect a like gift in return. In presentations, there are two ways this could apply. The first is to acknowledge and agree with the audience on their point of view, even if it is contrary to what you are trying to present. This lets them know that you agree with a potential issue or objection. You have something in common now. Using the principle of reciprocation, you then stand a better chance of getting their agreement to one of your points later, since you had concurred first with one of their issues.

The second application is related to being open in your presentation. Reciprocation also applies when we acknowledge a flaw in our argument or data. The audience would likely be more open to admitting a flaw in their viewpoint or feeling a greater sense of security in your opinion, since you had previously confessed to some misgivings yourself.

In both these applications, we are first giving the audience something that they did not ask or pay for and then increasing our chances of getting something of benefit in return, later on.

Principle of Commitment and Consistency: We act in order to be consistent with what we have committed to — even if it is destructive or does not make sense

Application for business presentations: There are three specific ways to apply this principle in our presentations. The first way is to look for some means to get the audience to agree with you in some minor fashion at the start of your presentation. Perhaps you ask them to agree that the objective you have outlined is shared. Then, when larger issues come up later in the presentation, you have a better chance of getting agreement, since they have already established a pattern of agreement with you.

The second application extends from the first. If you are making a presentation that builds to an overall conclusion, structure your presentation so that you get agreement on each building block of your argument as you proceed. Then, when you show how the pieces form the larger conclusion at the end of your presentation, the audience is more likely to agree with the conclusion since they have publicly agreed with each piece.

The final application is a visual design consideration. When creating your visuals, use an equation diagram as a way to illustrate how each of the building blocks they have agreed to results in the only logical conclusion that they can draw. More information on equation diagrams is found in chapter five.

Principle of Social Proof: One way to determine what is correct is to find out what other people think is correct. The principle applies especially to the way we decide what constitutes correct behaviour. We view a behaviour as more correct in a given situation to the degree that we see others performing it. The effect is greater when the people we are observing are similar to us.

Application for business presentations: This principle explains why we see so many presentations with overloaded text slides. Since we see colleagues or our bosses presenting this way, we might conclude that it is the correct way to present. Unfortunately, this is the wrong conclusion, but we experience few examples of better ways to present, which is a good reason to read this book.

We can apply this principle to our presentations by showing our audience examples of how people just like them have adopted our suggestions (whether it is a proposed decision or the purchase of a product or service). This gives the decision-makers a certain comfort level. If others like them have made the decision, it is most likely the right decision. Our proof can come in the form of testimonials and other examples, particularly ones that come from people that they would identify with, in similar positions, industries or circumstances.

Principle of Liking: We prefer to say "yes" to the requests of someone we know and like. This begs the question: What causes us to like someone? It helps:

- if there is some physical attractiveness,
- if they are similar in some ways to ourselves;
- if they are generous with compliments;
- if they are similar to someone we knew in the past;

- if they are working toward the same goals;
- if we are teammates or;
- if they are people we associate with good things/success.

Application for business presentations: This principle is backed up by a study that concluded that the nonverbal interaction of a presenter (making frequent eye contact, walking around the room vs. staying behind a podium, and seeming relaxed, friendly, and approachable) was considered more important than the use of technology when rating the trustworthiness and competence of a presenter. How can you apply this principle in your presentations? Here are some suggestions.

Before the presentation starts, spend time talking with audience members who arrive early. Ask their opinions and inquire about their experiences. During the presentation, refer to them by name and refer to their viewpoints and examples. Find common areas of interest with the audience and refer to these in your presentation. Pay attention to your attire for the presentation since this will influence the decision-makers view of your ideas.

Point out how you were once in a similar situation (if this is the case) and how you worked through the issues they are now struggling with. Associate yourself, through examples and stories, with those that the audience considers successful. All of these ideas will lead to the audience liking you more and result in a better chance that they will accept your ideas.

Principle of Authority: We have a deep-seated sense of duty to authority within all of us. There are three common symbols of authority: titles, clothes, and trappings.

Application for business presentations: This principle is easier to apply when you hold a superior organizational position than that of your audience, but in most situations this will not be the case;

you will need to apply it in different ways. Here are three suggestions:

First, you need to credibly position yourself as the expert on this topic. Factors in your favour include your educational background, relevant experience, including published material or media exposure as well as how others look up to you as the authoritative voice on this topic.

Second, you need to dress as an expert would dress. Look at the most respected authorities on your topic and dress accordingly.

Finally, use respected sources to back up your statements. Draw on academic research or quotes from well-known people in the field to lend more credibility to your ideas. This will help establish your authority and the authority of your ideas in the minds of the decision-makers.

Principle of Scarcity: Opportunities seem more valuable to us when their availability is limited. As opportunities become less available, we lose the freedom to make that choice. We hate to lose the freedoms we possess, so we will desire the privileges, and the associated goods and services that result from that freedom of choice even more.

The most powerful influence occurs when there is a sudden scarcity of an item that used to be abundant, especially if the scarcity has been driven by an increased demand for the item.

Application for business presentations: The most common application of this principle is the "limited time offer," where a benefit, whether it is a special price, feature or bonus item, is available only if the decision is made before a certain stated time limit.

This principle also applies when you can point out the benefit of acting quickly and the disadvantage of delaying a decision. This can help the audience resolve an issue and make a positive change quickly. Depending on the situation, you may also be able to show how future options or choices would be restricted if the decision was not made in a certain way or within a certain timeframe.

In applying any of these principles, it is important to understand that you should never use the knowledge of the principles to deceive or manipulate your audience. That would be very short-term thinking and is always destructive, whether we are found out or not.

Understanding these six principles of persuasion allows you to consider how to structure, design and deliver your presentation to more effectively persuade an audience of decision-makers.

In order to better understand persuasion, we turn next to the work of Chip and Dan Heath, who wrote the book "Made to Stick." This is a study of why some ideas stick in our minds, while others do not. They outline six key qualities of an idea that makes it stick in decision-makers' minds. They define a sticky idea as one that is understandable, memorable, and effective in changing thought or behaviour. They employ a mnemonic device to remember these six "sticky" qualities, using the acronym: SUCCESs. Here is a summary of their ideas with some suggestions on how we can use them to make each presentation stick in the minds of our audience.

Quality #1: Simplicity—Find the core of the idea.
Application for business presentations: Each idea that we present must be broken down to the essential core. When designing a

slide, this core idea should be the headline of the slide, stated in a way that relates to the audience. It should summarize what we want them to understand.

Quality #2: Unexpected—Get attention with something that surprises. Keep their attention by tapping into their natural curiosity.

Application for business presentations: At the start of the presentation, we need to grab the attention of the audience with something that is beyond their expectations. A startling statistic, an unexpected conclusion or an outrageous quote could jolt them. To keep their attention, we should structure our presentation so that we highlight a gap in their knowledge that causes them to be curious about what is missing.

Quality #3: Concrete—Examine with your senses.

Application for business presentations: To make our ideas more concrete for our audiences, we need to relate ideas in ways that are tangible, so the audience can touch, hear, see, taste or smell them. If we are presenting more abstract ideas, we need to translate them into ways the audience can relate to. In many cases, this leads to visuals that represent or illustrate the idea or situation.

Quality #4: Credible—Our belief in ideas is influenced by the honesty and trustworthiness of the source of the ideas or the support for the ideas. It is also impacted by whether or not we can relate the proof to our own situation.

Application for business presentations: If we are to influence our audiences through the message in a presentation, we need to ensure that the statistics and proof used comes from sources that the audience considers credible. It is also important to create analogies that the audience can relate to, based on the real world they know. This can transform potentially dry and unappealing statistics into a format that appeals to decision-makers. It also allows them to understand more clearly how it applies to their situation.

Quality #5: Emotional—People only act if they care about the idea. In order to care about an idea, people have to relate it to their own self-interest.

Application for business presentations: People care more about an issue or idea when they feel the impact on an individual level instead of a group level. In our presentations, we should help the audience "see" how the idea can improve their own future. Then there is a better chance that they will implement the idea.

This self-interest also has a downside that we need to be aware of. The Heath brothers call it The Curse of Knowledge— the assumption that the audience knows as much and cares as much about the topic as you do. This causes a presenter to want to share all the details and processes behind the ideas or information. When speaking with decision-makers, this curse causes you to talk over their heads or not give them a context or setting in which to relate the data to their own situation. The message is lost if the details overwhelm and the audience is left confused. Decision-makers care about what is important to them. Focus your presentation on their self-interest, not your own, if you want to successfully persuade them.

Quality #6: Stories—A story has power in relation to the simulation (knowledge about how to act in a situation) and inspiration (the motivation to act when in a similar situation) it provides.

Application for business presentations: Stories are one of the most powerful ways to deliver a persuasive presentation. But just randomly adding stories does not help your presentation. You must be deliberate in the choice of the story you use. The story must match the point you are making and be relevant to that audience. Once you have decided on which stories to use, practice telling the stories until they flow well. It should be clear to the audience how the story ties in to the point you are making. A well told story will be passed on and be remembered long after most of the rest of the presentation is forgotten.

Conclusion: Persuasive Visuals Work

It has been clear for years that most presentations can be made much more effective. The endless recitation of text displayed on the screen does not persuade decision-makers. Nevertheless, we can change this by tapping into the power of visuals. We can design the presentation and its visual support to take advantage of the power of the principles and application of persuasion. By doing so, we can create presentations that make an impact and influence others to make more informed decisions.

CHAPTER TWO

The KWICK Method for Creating Persuasive Visuals

In the previous chapter we have seen why persuasive visuals need to be used in presentations, but the natural questions are "What is a visual slide?" and "How do you create a persuasive visual?" This chapter defines a visual slide and gives an overview of a five-step method that you can use to create persuasive visuals of your own. Each step will then be explained in detail in the subsequent chapters.

What is a visual slide?

A number of commentators have suggested that the solution to overloaded text slides is to create only slides that contain no text. They suggest that by eliminating text, the problems with poor slides will be solved. But this advice is too short-sighted. It is important to know the two ends of the spectrum – all text or no text. But I do not think that either extreme represents the best option. A balance is more effective than either extreme. There is a role for text and visuals on slides.

Instead of defining a visual slide by what is absent, my definition is, "A visual slide is not the absence of text—it is the presence of a visual that encourages a conversation with the audience." Let me explain the parts of this definition.

The first part of the definition makes the point that it is not about a lack of words on the slide. It is more than that. The second part refers to the visual on the slide. This visual could be a picture, graph, diagram, illustration, media clip or other visual.

It does not relate to a specific type of visual, but merely that one is present on the slide, usually along with some text.

The last part of the definition is the key part. The visual you are using encourages the audience to think, consider your point, and engage in conversation with you, as the presenter. A good presentation is not a one-way communication. It occurs when the audience and presenter are engaged in a discussion of the ideas that are being presented. Involvement increases the level of caring the audience has with the ideas.

We will use this definition as the basis for our discussions in the rest of this book. Having a definition gives us parameters for our investigation of visual slides, but it does not provide clues as to HOW to create those slides.

What is the KWICK Method?

In my work with both individual presenters and within organizations in training groups of executives, I recognized that presenters liked the idea of creating visual slides, but did not have a simple process that would help them create the slides.

We are not usually inclined to think visually. We usually write our thoughts, which leads to putting paragraphs of text on to slides. We also think that to create visuals, we need some design and graphics training, which many of us do not have. In short, it looks difficult, so, expecting to fail, we do not attempt it.

Initially, making the move from text-overloaded slides to persuasive visuals can seem daunting. We are moving from our comfort zone to a new way of not only creating slides, but of using them in our presentations. There is a risk of failure—What if they laugh at my slides or, even worse, do not understand my message because it is not written out?

I suggest that the greater risk is not differentiating your presentation from all the others that the decision-makers are seeing. Not standing out and not being remembered will lead to greater failure.

The anticipated difficulty and fears can be overcome with the five-step process I introduce in this section. I developed this process by stepping back and examining what I go through to create slides for clients. I also looked at the principles of persuasion that we discussed in chapter one to see how those ideas would integrate with the process I already used. I discovered that there were five simple steps that would help presenters unleash the power of persuasive visuals in their own presentations.

The KWICK Method

The five steps are arranged as the acronym KWICK. It makes the steps easy to remember and apply. It also emphasizes that the process is neither long nor hard. The five KWICK steps are:

K   ey point
W   ords that suggest the visual
I   n context
C   rystal clear
K   eep focus

The next five chapters explain each of the steps in great detail, but let us look at an overview of what each step represents.

The first step is to get really clear regarding what the **Key Point** of the slide should be. Each slide should make one point and one point only. This first step articulates the key point for each slide. If you are not clear on the point of the slide, any visual you may create will be confusing. Analyze the data or other inputs and decide what the strongest point will be for this slide. It may be that your data leads to two or three important points. If so, you must create two or three slides, with one point for each. State your point as a sentence. The sentence does not have to be expressed in perfect grammar, but it should clearly state the conclusion you want the audience to draw from the slide. It will become the headline for your slide. In chapter three, we will look at the process for analyzing data to determine the key point, the difference between a title and a headline, and how to determine if your headline is the right length and structure.

Now that you know the key point, next, you should not only decide to use a visual, but determine which one. But how do you know what visual to create? You look at the **Words That Suggest The Visual**. Once you have written the headline for your slide, look at the words and phrases you used to summarize the key point.

These words will give you clues as to what type of visual will work best for this slide. If you talk about the trend of data, create a graph. If you wrote about a flow or process, use a diagram. Pay attention to the words and the best visuals will come to mind. Photos, diagrams, graphs, video clips or screen captures can be utilized. Get additional clues by listening to how you describe the point to others.

In chapter four we list common words and phrases to look for and what visuals each may suggest. This list will help you to see ideas and concepts you regularly present in a whole new way.

Once the type of visual has been selected, the next step is to create the visual. The most important part of creating the visual is to make certain that it is **In Context** for the audience. The audience must be able to relate to the visual to become engaged with the message. When creating visuals for your slides, represent your idea in such a way that the audience will be able to understand your point. This goes back to some of the core persuasion principles. Perhaps you need to compare it to something they are familiar with. It may be that you have to present it at a high level because they do not want to be swamped with details that are not relevant to them. In chapter five, we go into considerable detail about how to create the different visuals that you will most likely use on your slides. Visuals such as graphs, diagrams, photographs and media clips are covered. For each visual, examples of a typical text slide and a more persuasive visual are shown. Then we discuss the best design practices for each type of visual.

After the visual has been created, your next step is to make sure the point is **Crystal Clear**. Message clarity is paramount to a successful presentation; the point of the visual must be easily understood. Methods for improving the clarity include:

- The proper use of well-designed callouts containing both graphics and text to direct the audience's attention to the most important part of the visual;
- The use of photos embedded in graphs or diagrams to further enliven the point;
- The use of shading in some pictures or graphics to emphasize certain areas—by having surrounding areas fade out to the background.

Chapter six covers each of these techniques in detail and explains what they add to your visual.

Once the slides have been created, It's Showtime! All your hard work in creating the slides will be wasted unless you **Keep** the **Focus** of the audience where you want it to be. As you are presenting, the audience can get easily confused. The visual must be presented in a logical manner that keeps their attention on the conclusion you want them to draw from each slide. Chapter seven covers techniques, such as:

- building the elements of your slides, piece-by-piece;
- breaking down complex diagrams or examples;
- using advanced techniques that allow the audience to dictate the order of topics and;
- presenting to audiences in different locations at once through web presentation services.

At the end of each chapter, you will see the ideas applied to two example slides—one from a sales-type presentation and the other from a current situation update-type presentation. These slide makeover examples will build throughout each chapter, so you can see the creation process applied to one slide the whole way through. Here are the two example slides as they were originally designed.

Slide Makeover Examples

Example #1: Sales Presentation Slide

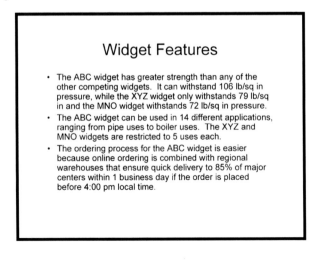

This is a typical sales presentation slide, listing features of the product. It is overloaded with text and the message is muddled. We will transform this slide into a persuasive visual using the KWICK method.

Example #2: Current Situation Slide

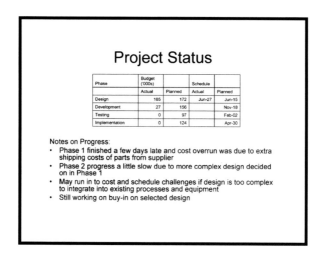

Project Status

Phase	Budget ('000s)		Schedule	
	Actual	Planned	Actual	Planned
Design	185	172	Jun-27	Jun-15
Development	27	156		Nov-18
Testing	0	97		Feb-02
Implementation	0	124		Apr-30

Notes on Progress:
- Phase 1 finished a few days late and cost overrun was due to extra shipping costs of parts from supplier
- Phase 2 progress a little slow due to more complex design decided on in Phase 1
- May run in to cost and schedule challenges if design is too complex to integrate into existing processes and equipment
- Still working on buy-in on selected design

This is a typical slide used in internal presentations to update executives about the current status of a project or initiative. It includes a spreadsheet and text, with the key message buried in the slide somewhere.

Decisions need to be made, but the decision-maker will not easily understand what is being presented and what decision they are being asked to consider. A clear visual slide will emerge after the KWICK method is applied.

There is no longer a need to feel intimidated when creating persuasive visuals. This role is no longer restricted to those who have advanced training in graphic design. You can apply the KWICK method to your next presentation and create persuasive visuals that will be effective. Decision-makers will sit up and take action.

CHAPTER THREE

Key Point

The first step in creating persuasive visuals is to decide on the key point that you want to make. Too often, presenters simply report all the data and hope that the decision-makers can find the point. This results in confusing the decision-makers, which means the presentation has been a failure.

I tell presenters that they need to tune their radio to station WIMTT. It is available in every local area, but most presenters do not listen to it. The call letters stand for What It Means To Them and the radio is the one you listen to in your head, not available on the FM band. When thinking about the key point, think about it from the perspective of the audience, not from your own point of view.

Sometimes the key point is obvious, but many times you need to consider a set of data or a situation that exists and figure out what the key point is. Make no mistake—the responsibility for figuring out the key point lies with you, the presenter, not with your audience. Here is a six-step process for analyzing data in order to determine the key point.

The Data Analysis Process

Step One: Create Your Expectation

Just like in any scientific research, you first need to determine what you expect the analysis to show. If you do not have an expectation, you should question whether the analysis is worth doing, since you will not know how to proceed. It is best to test your expectation for reasonableness. You can do so by using previous outcomes or similar situations from other areas of the organization, other organizations, external reports or industry publications. Note any concerns you have about the logic of your argument because they may become explanations in later stages of the analysis.

There are usually two types of expectations that you will use:

- Like/Not like a specific value or trend. With this expectation, you have concluded that your data should be either similar or dissimilar to a known value or trend based on specific reasons. We see this often with economic data where, for example, housing starts are expected to be an approximate value, based on what experts feel happened in that market the previous month, or the same month last year. We see trend expectations for example, when we hear that profits in a certain industry are expected to reverse a trend seen over the last year due to a regulatory change. When you set an expectation based on a value or trend, always record why you are selecting that value or trend and on what basis you are doing so (such as published reports or other research).

- Correlated with another variable. This expectation suggests that the topic you are analyzing is correlated in some way—positively or negatively—with a specific variable. You must have some reason for making this expectation and those reasons should be recorded. One example of an expectation being correlated with a variable is the number of vehicle accidents increasing later in the day. In this case, we expect that as people get tired later in the day and at night, accidents would increase.

Step Two: Determine Data Needed

Once you have created your expectation, you can now determine what specific data you need in order to test against the expectation. Be as specific as you can about the data you need. List any breakdowns of the data you need by geography, time, category, age range, gender or other relevant criteria. The more specific you can be on the data you need, the easier it will be to locate the data, and the less time will be spent massaging the data. This will make for a more robust and accurate analysis.

If we continue with the vehicle accidents example from Step One, we would specify the data as clearly as possible. For example, we may want to find vehicle accident data in the four surrounding counties in the past twelve month period. If you can be very specific about the data, this makes it easier in the next step to find the data that we need.

Step Three: Collect the Data

Once you have a list of the data you need, it is time to collect the data. Research what sources you have available and rank each source as to the reliability of the data from that source. Look at what data you have available internally and consider how that data gets created. Determine as well, any reliability issues that may exist. Well-respected external sources, such as government statistics bureaus, universities and major private research firms have documented procedures to ensure their data are reliable.

See how the source breaks down the data and compare that to how you need to analyze it. Also, check the cost of the data that you need. If you have a choice, you should prefer to receive the data in electronic format, such as a comma delimited file or spreadsheet-type file. This will make the data much easier to manipulate and it will reduce or eliminate transcription errors that occur when printed data is manually entered into a computer system.

It is also a good idea to determine how you will test the validity of the data that you receive. Spot checks on random data values are a good way to see if there has been any keying or collection error on the part of the source organization.

In our vehicle accident example, we would look for the specific data from a police or government agency to ensure greater accuracy and we would prefer to get the data as a database or spreadsheet extract in order to be able to work with it more easily.

Step Four: Perform Analysis

With the data in hand, you can now begin analyzing it. Spreadsheets and statistical tools are usually used to calculate values and trends from the data. Double-check all formulas and calculations to make sure that the results look reasonable. If a calculated value stands out, it may be due to an error in a formula or an error in copying or retyping values. Once your calculations are complete, compare the results to the expectation that you set in step one. Consider both the absolute difference and relative difference between the result and the expectation. Sometimes the absolute difference may be small (such as finding a result of 23.4 when you were expecting 26.7), but the relative difference as expressed as a percent may be more important (in the previous example an absolute difference of 3.3 is a 12.4% difference).

For our vehicle accident example, we would break down the data by hour during the day and look at the average number of accidents in each hour. The resulting averages could be graphed to determine if there is a correlation or not.

Step Five: Draw Conclusions

This is the critical step in determining the key point from a set of data. In this step, you need to consider what the analysis and comparison to the expectation mean in the context of your presentation. A lower trend than expected may suggest that your expansion expectations may need to be reconsidered if product demand will not be as strong as first anticipated. A higher than expected order backlog may indicate a need to investigate process improvements to increase productivity in the production area.

As a specialist, you will have to use a strategic view of the situation. The question you must ask yourself is: What are the most important conclusions derived from the analysis of the trends and statistics? The answer to this question will form the heart of what the decision-makers need to hear from your work.

If there is a large difference between your result and your expectation, you may need to consider whether the original expectation was reasonable. You may revisit the original work in coming up with the expectation in step one and decide to change that expectation based on new information.

After we examined the data in our vehicle accident example, we may conclude that indeed, there is a correlation between time of day and number of accidents, but perhaps not the correlation that we thought. It seems that certain times of day have more accidents, but there is no evidence of a steady progression during the day.

Step 6: Explain Differences

When there are significant differences between the result of your analysis and your expectation that are not explained by simple timing or other regular variance issues, you need to explain the differences to the executives. This is answering the "Why?" question. "Why does the analysis show the result it does?" If you cannot explain the differences with good reasoning, the decision-makers will make up their own explanations, which may or may not have any basis in reality. But once they become convinced of an explanation, they will make decisions based on it. Thus, it is far better to give them the explanation initially instead of them making up their own.

The final step in our vehicle accident example is to explain why the correlation was different than we expected. It may be that the number of accidents is really a factor of how much traffic there is on the roads and it just happens that traffic is heavier at certain times of the day. We could then create another expectation and gather data to test it in order to confirm our point.

Writing the Slide Headline

Once your analysis or contemplation has determined the key point of the slide, it is time to write the headline of the slide. I am deliberate in my choice of that word—headline. The text at the top of a slide is typically referred to as the title of the slide. But a title does not serve your audience as well as a headline does. Let us look at the differences between a title and a headline.

Title	Headline
Usually 2-4 words in length	Typically 6-10 words long
Too short to give anything more than the topic	Structured as a sentence that gives a complete thought
Does not help audience determine meaning	Clearly states key point of the slide to communicate with the audience

In newspapers and magazines, they do not have titles, but headlines for the different stories. If they only had titles, people would be discouraged from reading further because they would not know what to expect from their further investment of time. Writers and editors create headlines that pique the curiosity of readers who must learn more—so they dive into the rest of the article or story. When creating headlines for your slides, think as a journalist would when creating a headline.

Work to avoid what we see far too often on presentation slides—the same title on every slide. What the presenter has done is used a topic area as the title or, even worse, the presentation title as the title for every slide. The audience is left trying to figure out what the point of each slide is.

Here are some tips that work well in creating headlines for slides:

1. Create a sentence as the headline. This ensures that you have a noun and a verb that make sense with other descriptors.

2. Choose your verbs and adjectives carefully. Have a bias towards active verbs and descriptive phrases. Avoid passive verbs.

3. Consider the tense of the verb(s) you use. Make sure that the verb tense is accurate for the point you are making— past, present or future.

4. Do not feel bound by the formal rules of grammar. While your headline will have a basic sentence structure, do not feel that you have to follow every grammar school rule. This is a sales tool. You are selling a point of view.

5. Keep it from six to ten words long so it can fit into two lines at the top of the slide.

6. It is okay to replace words with punctuation. You can replace the word "and" with an ampersand (&) or a semi-colon (;) in order to join two thoughts.

7. Use sentence case. Do not capitalize every word in the headline (you would not in a regular sentence). Capitalize the first word, any word after a semi-colon and key words or proper names.

8. To keep it short, use numbers instead of writing the number out. Use "3" instead of "three."

9. In most cases, headlines will be centered on the slide unless the slide design has other formatting.
10. If necessary, insert a line break to keep important words together. Learn how to insert a line break instead of a paragraph break in your slide software.
11. Do not include a period at the end of the headline, it is unnecessary.
12. In most cases, forms of the verb "to be" can be omitted when writing a headline. For example, write "increased competition coming" instead of "increased competition is coming."
13. Be careful about using jargon or abbreviations that decision-makers may not be familiar with. Use words or phrases they can relate to.
14. Make every word count. You are restricted to very few words to make the point. Feel free to drop articles such as "a" or "the" when needed.

Remember that determining the key point of your slide is your job, not the job of the audience. Do the work to determine the most important point, then write a headline that clearly states that key point for the decision-makers.

Slide Makeover Examples

Example #1: Sales Presentation Slide

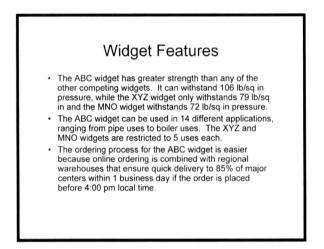

One of the problems in determining the key point on this slide is that the presenter has actually included three points on the slide. This is a common mistake and is easily corrected by making a separate slide for each point. For our purposes, we will only deal with the first point the presenter is trying to make.

When looking at what the presenter included in the first bullet point on the slide, we see that there is some test data which supports a conclusion that the ABC widget is stronger than the other two competing products. You would want to check the data to verify the reliability of the source and the accuracy of the quoted data. Is the strength of this product a relevant attribute that the potential customer would care about? If not, this point should not be included in the presentation.

Once the verification of the data is complete, we can then create the new slide headline. We want it to be short, but capture the key point. "ABC Widget is the strongest on the market" would be a good headline. It captures the key point and is written as a sentence of eight words. We will start the creation of our revised slide with this headline.

Example #2: Current Situation Presentation Slide

Project Status

Phase	Budget ('000s)		Schedule	
	Actual	Planned	Actual	Planned
Design	185	172	Jun-27	Jun-15
Development	27	156		Nov-18
Testing	0	97		Feb-02
Implementation	0	124		Apr-30

Notes on Progress:
- Phase 1 finished a few days late and cost overrun was due to extra shipping costs of parts from supplier
- Phase 2 progress a little slow due to more complex design decided on in Phase 1
- May run in to cost and schedule challenges if design is too complex to integrate into existing processes and equipment
- Still working on buy-in on selected design

The challenge when a slide contains numeric data is to determine whether the key point is contained in the numeric data shown or whether further work needs to be done in order to figure out what the most important point is. In this slide, the table of numbers and dates does not seem to be sufficient to draw the conclusions we need.

The text and the data seem to suggest that this project could be challenging on three counts: the cost, the schedule and the buy-in from staff. But you would need to go back to the data and prepare projections of the current situation in order to determine which of these three areas will pose the greatest challenge for this project. With the current trends in the data, you should be able to project a new anticipated cost and projected finish date. These can then be compared to the original planned cost and date. The buy-in issue is trickier since it does not only involve numeric projections, but will probably require interviews and process analysis.

In this example, we will select the buy-in issue as the most important and create a headline that brings this issue to the attention of the decision-makers. A headline like "Complex Selected Design Causing Challenges in Buy-In" will raise the flag about the issue that the presenter needs some help in addressing. It is seven words long and makes the key point clearly. We will use this headline as we move to the next step of considering the visual that would best represent the key point.

CHAPTER FOUR

Words That Suggest the Visual

The words from the slide headline and how you will talk about the key point will give you clues as to what visual will work best for this slide. Many presenters think that they need training in graphic design or they need to be a "creative" type to come up with visuals. Not at all.

When you start to tune your radar to the words and phrases used to describe the key point, you will often see the correct visual almost jump out at you. Many of the words or phrases will suggest how the ideas are organized, compared or related to each other. Take these clues and solve the puzzle of the appropriate visual for this point. Use the list of words and phrases below to start to train your mental radar.

One slide makeover that I did illustrates this step well. The original slide came from an accounting professor. It had been used to explain the five stages that stock goes through in a corporation. The original slide contained only text and was likely read word-for-word to the class. I recognized that there were two dimensions from the words used. First, there was a time dimension and second it seemed important if the stock was inside or outside the corporation. So I redesigned the slide as a diagram which showed a stock certificate moving from inside to outside the corporation along a timeline. After the professor saw the revised slide, they started using it to explain the concepts because the new slide was much more effective.

Words & Phrases that suggest a visual

The table below lists words and phrases that you can identify and the clues they provide in selecting a visual. Do not use this as a restrictive list, limiting your selection to only the suggestions given in the table. Use it as a starting point that can lead you in the right direction, sometimes quickly and sometimes through a more involved pathway. In the next chapter, you will see examples of the types of visuals suggested in the table and a list of best practices for creating each one.

Word/Phrase	Clues to the appropriate visual
Market share	Used when comparing the portion of one segment to the whole; suggests a pie chart as a possible visual
Percentage	Not always a definitive clue; look for context and what the percentage refers to; could suggest graphs or diagrams
Share of, Portion, Slice, Part of	Similar to market share; suggests pie chart or diagram if share/portion is not numeric
Trend	Usually based on numeric data; suggests a graph
Survey results	Most common visual for survey results is a reverse stairstep bar graph with the longest bar at the top
Comparison, comparing, contrasting	Usually one of multiple clues needed; could suggest a table of attributes, diagram or sometimes a graph

Results in	Shows causal relationship; usually suggests a diagram
… over time	Time based relationship; suggests Gantt chart or timeline diagram; if numeric results, could suggest column, line or mountain graphs
… among departments, between departments	Relationship between parts of an organization or comparing results from organizations; suggests diagram if showing relationship and graph if showing results
Related, Relationship between	Clue tells you there is a relationship, but not what type; look for additional clues nearby to determine type or nature of relationship
Sum of, Calculated by	There is some sort of mathematical relationship between different parts; suggests an equation diagram
Difference between	Could be similar to sum of, but could also be similar to comparison of attributes; could suggest an equation diagram, other diagram or table
Flow	There is a sequence or direction; suggests a flow or arrow diagram
Process	Usually a sequence of steps with different possible paths; suggests a process map or flow diagram
Procedure	Can refer to decisions or authority; could suggest diagrams or photos

Steps in ...	Usually similar to process, but could also be steps in a decision; suggests process map, flow diagram or decision tree diagram
Options	Often related to making a decision; suggests decision tree or other diagram; could suggest a table if comparing attributes of the option
Subordinate, Hierarchy	Indicates a hierarchical relationship; suggests a hierarchical diagram
Break down, decompose	Usually showing parts of a whole; could suggest a diagram, but could also suggest a pie graph
Assemble, disassemble	Shows how parts go together or come apart; suggests a diagram or photos
Dimensions	Commonly used when describing an object; suggests a photo or diagram
Inside/outside	Can refer to relationship between entities; suggests a diagram and photos of the entities
Timeline	Time-based relationship; suggests Gantt chart or timeline diagram
Geographic, specific geographic locations	Information is correlated with geographic area; suggests map
Name of a place, location, event, object, product, service or person	Suggests a photo to give context
Story about a person/situation	Suggests photo(s) to give context and sequence

Demonstration	Used to show how something is done; suggests series of photos or video clip
Testimonial	Used as third party proof of a claim or statement; suggests photo of person, audio clip or video clip
Illustration, illustrating	Usually showing a point through a photo, drawing or video clip
Example, show	Is a partial clue; look for other words or phrases that give additional clues as to what type of example this is
Screen shot, screen capture	Used to show an example from a computer screen or other screen displaying information; suggests a screen capture image or a photo
Table of ...	Related to comparison usually; suggests table but look for other clues that may suggest different visual
Position, Rank	Usually hierarchical relationship; suggests hierarchical diagram
Levels, Components	Commonly used in hierarchy or component relationships; suggests a diagram
If this ... then ..., When this ... then ...	Causal relationship; suggests arrow diagram
x number of parts	Can be similar to components, but could also be parts of a whole; suggests diagram or pie chart
Parameters	Usually attributes of an item; suggests a table

...est words (i.e. largest, strongest, etc.), ...er words (i.e. lighter, greater, etc.)	Rank of items based on a criteria; usually suggests a graph to show the differences in the measured criteria

The above list is by no means exhaustive; you will likely have words and phrases or suggestions of visuals that you would want added to this table. Feel free to add to the table from your own experience (and e-mail me your suggestions if you would be kind enough to share them).

Once you have decided on the most appropriate visual for the slide, you can proceed to the next section, where we cover how to create that visual, keeping it in context for the audience.

Slide Makeover Examples

Example #1: Sales Presentation Slide

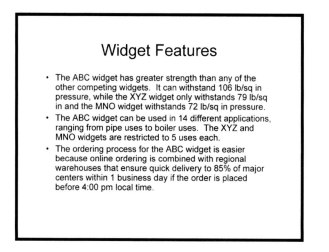

We need to look for clues to the appropriate visual in our headline "ABC Widget is the strongest on the market" and in the text that the presenter originally used to describe the strength.

One clue comes from the word "greater" in the explanatory text. Any word ending in "…er" is a comparison word and, using the table above, it is one clue, but usually this is not sufficient to give us the answer. Another clue is that we see numbers in the text and a comparison of numbers usually suggests a graph. The third clue is the word "strongest" in the headline. This also suggests a comparison. These clues definitely point to using a graph as the visual. The specific type of graph would be a column graph because it could show the comparison in measured strength between the three competing products.

By following the clues found in the way the presenter is describing the point they want to make, we have been able to decide on using a column graph to show how the ABC widget is stronger than the competition. In the next chapter we will create the column graph.

Example #2: Current Situation Presentation Slide

Project Status

Phase	Budget ('000s)		Schedule	
	Actual	Planned	Actual	Planned
Design	185	172	Jun-27	Jun-15
Development	27	156		Nov-18
Testing	0	97		Feb-02
Implementation	0	124		Apr-30

Notes on Progress:
• Phase 1 finished a few days late and cost overrun was due to extra shipping costs of parts from supplier
• Phase 2 progress a little slow due to more complex design decided on in Phase 1
• May run in to cost and schedule challenges if design is too complex to integrate into existing processes and equipment
• Still working on buy-in on selected design

From our last look at this slide, we saw that there were three possible issues that the presenter wanted to highlight: cost, schedule and buy-in. We assumed that the most important issue is that of buy-in to the changes. In that case, we will look for clues on how to best show this issue visually. The clues needed to determine a visual for this slide start with the phrase "run into" in the third bullet point. This is a future time clue and suggests that we should use a visual that can show the decision-makers what the future situation could look like. We also see the word "processes" in the same bullet point. This strong clue suggests that a process diagram would be a good visual to use since it could depict what the future state would be and the anticipated problems.

Again, by using the clues provided in the way we describe the key point, we have determined that we will need to create a process map diagram to show where the challenges are going to occur and the reasons that those changes are causing an issue with staff buy-in. In the next chapter we will create the process diagram.

CHAPTER FIVE

In Context

This step in the KWICK method is called In Context because the most important factor in creating the visual is to give it context so that the audience can look at it and immediately understand the meaning of the visual. Too often, visuals are created without context and it leads to confusion or even the wrong conclusion being drawn about the visual.

One visual that a client brought to me had many different elements on it, representing different parts of a process and different areas of the organization. It was overwhelming and very confusing to the audience. We redesigned the visual to be clear and clean, making the main point easy to understand.

Context ties back to our ability to persuade because if the audience cannot identify with the visual and does not find it familiar enough, they will not trust that they are making the right decision. Sometimes context is created by comparing an item or an idea to something they are familiar with. Sometimes it can be created by using a format they are used to seeing and sometimes we have to associate our visual through an analogy. There are other ways to create context, of course, but the key is to create a visual that is easy for this audience to understand.

This chapter is organized by the type of information you are creating a visual for:
- numeric information;
- processes or flows;
- relationships;
- organizing/comparing items;
- sharing a story or example;
- showing time-based information;

- geographic information and
- computer-based information.

Each section will give examples of why that type of visual is more effective than text, which sub-types should be used in which situations, the best practices for creating that type of visual and a list of steps to take when creating such a graphic.

To Present Numeric Information

When presenting numbers, the temptation is to copy a huge table of numbers from a spreadsheet and drop it onto a slide. Big mistake. Instead, use a graph to illustrate the point of all those numbers. If you do need to show a table of numbers, keep it to a reasonable size and highlight the important numbers. In this section, we will cover when to use different types of graphs, such as pie charts, line or mountain charts, column charts, and bar charts, as well as proper treatment of a table of numbers.

To show parts of a whole or percentages, use a Pie Chart

If you are discussing market share, percentage of a whole or any idea whereby you want to talk about how one part relates to other parts that make a whole, use a pie chart. Here is an example of a pie chart used instead of a text slide.

Text Slide   *Visual*

Our lagging market share

- Our company has 25% market share
- Company C has 34% market share
- Company J has 41% market share

Our lagging market share

Company J, 41%

Our company, 25%

Company C, 34%

When creating a pie chart, keep the following best practices in mind:

- Use 2-D instead of 3-D pie charts because the third dimension adds nothing to the understanding of the chart.
- Label each slice of the pie instead of using a legend because it is easier to understand and interpret.
- If you are discussing only one of the slices, use a color to fill in the slice you want to talk about and leave the other slices just in outline.
- Put the most important pie slice in the "12 o'clock" position of the pie.
- Explode or slightly separate the pie slice you want to discuss from the rest of the slices so it stands out.

To show trends in a large amount of data,
use a Line or Mountain Graph

When talking about trends in more than eight data points, it is best to use a line graph because it will show the trend visually. Here is an example of a line chart used instead of a text data table.

Text Slide   *Visual*

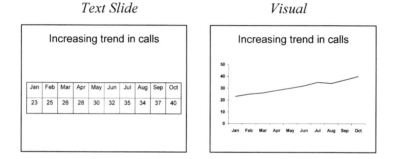

A mountain graph is a line graph that has the area below the line filled in with a contrasting color. Some people prefer mountain graphs if they find the line in a line graph hard to see.

When creating a line or mountain graph, keep the following best practices in mind:

- Minimize the number of labels on the vertical axis so that it is not so text-dense (dense text draws attention to the axis and away from the meaning of the graph).
- Eliminate any default legends created by the software and instead label each line if there is more than one line on the graph.
- Increase the line thickness of the data line to the maximum so it can be clearly seen.

- Choose the line graph format that does not have markers for each data point because the markers draw attention from the trend.
- Arrange the data in chronological or another meaningful order.
- Clear any horizontal grid lines that are added by default so that the graph stands out from the background.
- Clear any plot area border that is added by default to place more emphasis on the line in the graph.
- Always start the vertical axis at zero so that the relative difference between the data points is accurate and you are not exaggerating the difference.
- For mountain graphs, choose a color that contrasts with the background for the color that fills in below the line. You may want to select a different color than the line so that both stand out.

To show trends in a small amount of data,
use a Column Graph

When talking about trends in data with seven or fewer data points, it is best to use a column graph instead of a line graph because it shows the trend more dramatically than a line graph. Here is an example of a column graph used instead of a text data table.

Text Slide   *Visual*

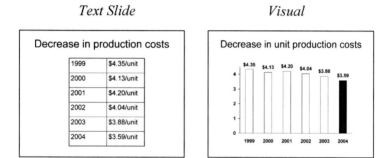

When creating a column graph, keep the following best practices in mind:

- Use 2-D instead of 3-D column graphs because the third dimension does not add to the understanding of the graph.
- Label each column instead of using a legend because it is easier to understand and interpret. You can add text labels vertically in the columns instead of above each column to save space and focus the attention on the graph instead of the labels.
- If you are discussing only one of the columns, use a color to fill in the column you want to talk about and leave the other columns just in outline.

- If necessary, add data labels to show the values of the columns.
- Clear the horizontal grid lines that may be added by default so that the graph stands out from the background.
- Clear the plot area border that may be added by default to place more emphasis on the columns in the graph.
- Arrange the data in chronological or another meaningful order.
- Minimize the number of labels on the vertical axis so that it is not so text-dense (dense text draws attention to the axis and away from the meaning of the graph).
- Always start the vertical axis at zero so that the relative difference is accurate and you are not exaggerating the difference between the columns.
- If you are using data labels that contain the value of each column, consider eliminating the vertical axis as it does not add any new information for the audience.
- Make the columns as wide as possible so that they are easy to see.

To show rank of items,
use a Bar Chart

When talking about data that is not chronological or arranged in some specific sequence, you are talking about the rank of each item relative to some ranking criteria. In these situations, use a bar chart to show the differences in rank. Here is an example of a bar chart used instead of a text slide.

Text Slide   *Visual*

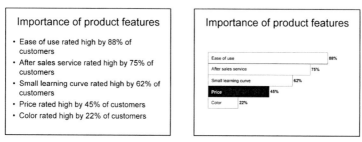

When creating a bar chart, keep the following best practices in mind:

- Use 2-D instead of 3-D bar charts because the third dimension does not add to the understanding of the chart.

- Label each bar instead of using a legend because it is easier to understand and interpret. These labels are best added by using separate text boxes placed on top of each bar in the chart after the chart has been formatted.

- If you are discussing only one of the bars, use a color to fill in the bar you want to talk about and leave the other bars just in outline.

- If necessary, add data labels to show the values of the bars.

- Clear the vertical grid lines that may be added by default so that the chart stands out from the background.
- Clear the plot area border that may be added by default to place more emphasis on the bars in the chart.
- Arrange the data in rank order or in some other meaningful order.
- Minimize the number of labels on the horizontal axis so that it is not so text-dense (dense text draws attention to the axis and away from the meaning of the graph). If you are using data labels to show values, you can often eliminate the horizontal axis altogether.
- If you are using a horizontal axis, always start the axis at zero so that the relative difference is accurate and you are not exaggerating the difference between the bars.

To show a table of numbers,
focus on the key ones

Sometimes you must show a table of numbers, either in addition to, or instead of, a graphical representation of that data. The key when showing a table is to make sure you focus the attention of the audience on the one number or a few numbers that are most important. Not all the numbers in the table are of equal importance—most are there just to give context. Make sure you know which ones are the truly important numbers.

When creating a table of numbers, keep the following best practices in mind:

- Try to restrict the table to no more than six columns by six rows. When large tables are displayed, the size of the text is hard to read and the audience will be overwhelmed trying to figure it out.

- Make sure that there are descriptive titles for each row and column.

- Add lines to divide the table of numbers so that it is easier to interpret.

- Highlight only the key numbers by using font size, font color or callouts (more on callouts in a later section).

- To enhance focus, shade out the other numbers once you focus on the key ones by using semi-transparent shapes to "dim" the non-focused numbers in the table.

- If you have a large table of numbers, break it down into sections and present each section individually. If you need to put the sections in context, use the "Break Down & Zoom In" technique described in a later section.

To Present Process or Flow

Many times a process or sequence is presented in a text slide with each step numbered (using numbers instead of bullets). You can do better. If you are showing the flow of information between departments, the manufacturing process for a particular product or a continuous improvement process in a high quality area, a diagram is the way to go. In this section we will cover creating flow diagrams for linear flows, continuous processes and multi-step decision diagrams.

To show a linear process or flow, use a Box and Arrow Diagram

If you are talking about a process or flow that is linear from a starting point to an ending point, use a box and arrow diagram to show the process or flow instead of a numbered or bulleted text list. Here is an example of a box and arrow diagram used instead of a numbered list text slide.

Text Slide   *Visual*

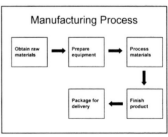

When creating a box and arrow diagram, keep the following best practices in mind:

- Use the software's drawing tools to create the shapes instead of a separate graphics program so that it is easier to change in the future.
- Increase the line thickness of any shape to at least three points so it is easy to see.
- To add text inside a shape, create a separate text box and drag it on to the shape to give yourself more formatting options for the text. Make sure to select a text color that contrasts with the fill color of the shape so the text can be seen.
- Use the graphic arrows in the software instead of the line arrows because they have better presence on the slide and are easier to see. Use a solid fill color for the arrows so they stand out.
- If you have created a complex diagram, use the "break down and zoom in" technique described in a later section when presenting it.
- To make the diagram even stronger, visually, you can fill each shape with a picture of the step being illustrated. This gives the audience an even better understanding of what the process step is.

Example of flow diagram with pictures for each step

To show a continuous process,
use a Circle Diagram

If you are talking about a process that is continuous, meaning that the first step starts again after the last step is complete, use a circle diagram instead of a text list of steps. Here is an example of a circle diagram used instead of a bulleted list text slide.

Text Slide   *Visual*

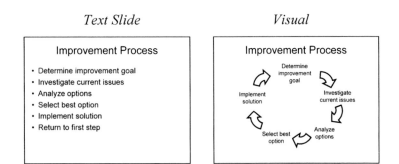

When creating a circle diagram, keep the following best practices in mind:

- Use the software's drawing tools to create the shapes instead of a separate graphics program so that it is easier to change in the future.
- Use an outlined arrow or a muted color for the arrow so it does not draw attention away from the steps in the process. The outlined arrow should have a line thickness of at least three points.
- The first step in the process should be at the twelve o'clock position in the circle.

- If you have more than six steps, consolidate them so that there are no more than six or the diagram will be too crowded.
- Use a large enough font for the text so that it stands out from the arrows.
- To make the diagram even stronger visually, you can add a picture of each step in the diagram and move the text below the picture (similar to the example on page 63 which shows pictures instead of shapes used for a flow diagram).

To show the sequence of decisions,
use a Decision Tree

If you are talking about items that are organized depending on previous decisions or choices, use a decision tree instead of long explanations. Here is an example of a decision tree used instead of a nested bullet list.

Text Slide   *Visual*

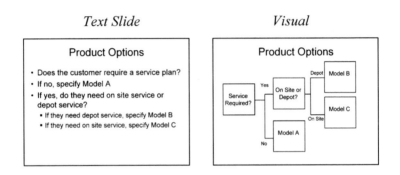

When creating a decision tree, keep the following best practices in mind:

- Use the software's line and box drawing tools to create the diagram instead of a separate graphics program so that it is easier to change in the future.
- Increase the line thickness of each line to at least 2.25 points so the line is easy to see.
- To add text inside a square or a chart, create a separate text box and drag it on to the diagram to give yourself more formatting options for the text.
- Set the font size of any text large enough so that it can be seen as easily as text on any other slide.
- Boil down the text of the decision question to only the key choices available at that decision box.

- Label each line in the decision tree so that the audience knows the direction for each choice and what result it will lead to.
- To make the decision tree even stronger, visually, you can fill each end result box with a picture of that result and put the text beside the box (similar to the example on page 63 which shows pictures instead of shapes used for a flow diagram). This gives the audience an even better understanding of what the final outcome is for each path in the tree.

To Show Relationships

Relationships are much better illustrated than explained in text form. Too often the text becomes far too wordy and almost impossible for an audience to follow. In this section we'll cover diagrams that show hierarchical relationships, overlapping relationships and causal relationships.

To show hierarchical relationships, use an Organization Chart

If you are talking about items that are organized in a hierarchical manner, use an organization chart instead of a text list. Here is an example of an organization chart used instead of a text list.

Text Slide   *Visual*

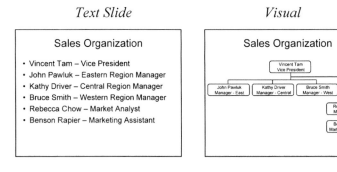

When creating an organization chart, keep the following best practices in mind:

- Use the software's line and box drawing tools to create the diagram instead of a separate graphics program or a built-in organization chart tool so that it is easier to change in the future.

- Consider using different types of boxes, such as square corner rectangles and rounded corner rectangles to distinguish between levels or other distinctions.
- Increase the line thickness of each line to at least 2.25 points so the line is easy to see.
- Format lines to represent different types of relationships, such as solid lines or dashed lines to distinguish between direct and indirect relationships.
- To add text inside a square, create a separate text box and drag it on to the diagram to give yourself more formatting options for the text.
- Set the font size of any text large enough so that it can be seen as easily as text on any other slide.
- To make the organization chart even stronger, visually, you can fill each box with a picture of the person and put the text underneath the picture. This gives the audience a face to go with the name and creates a much stronger personal connection.

To show overlapping relationships,
use a Venn Diagram

When you are talking about how two items have some aspects in common and other aspects are different, use a Venn diagram instead of a text list or chart. Here is an example of a Venn diagram used instead of a text list.

Text Slide   *Visual*

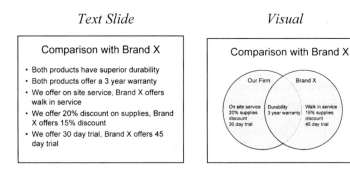

When creating a Venn diagram, keep the following best practices in mind:

- Use the software's drawing tools to create the shapes instead of a separate graphics program so that it is easier to change in the future.

- Increase the line thickness of each circle to at least 2.25 points so the outline of the circle is easy to see.

- To add text inside a circle, create a separate text box and drag it onto the circle to give yourself more formatting options for the text. Make sure to select a text color that contrasts with the fill color of the circle so the text can be seen.

- Set the transparency of the fill color for each circle (except the bottom circle) to 20-30% so that the overlapping can be seen but it is not so transparent that the text gets washed out.

- Select fill colors for the different circles that have enough contrast with each other so that each circle is distinct and the attributes that only apply to that circle are easily distinguished from the common attributes.
- When overlapping the circles, the circles should build in a clockwise manner, meaning that the circle farthest back in the diagram layers should be at the nine o'clock position and the rest of the circles should be layered on top in a clockwise direction.
- Make sure that each circle has a title either inside one side of the circle or just outside the circle so that it is easy to tell the different circles apart.

To show causal relationships,
use an Arrow Diagram

When you are talking about the relationship between an event and an outcome, use an arrow diagram to show the direction of the relationship. Here is an example of an Arrow diagram used instead of a text slide.

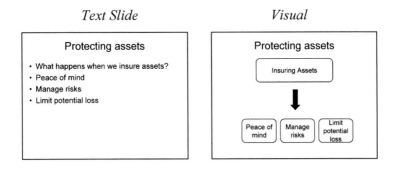

When creating an Arrow diagram, keep the following best practices in mind:

- Keep the diagram simple. If there are many causes and outcomes, group them so that the diagram has no more than three of either causes or outcomes.
- Construct the diagram vertically so that the cause is at the top and the outcome is at the bottom.
- Use the software's drawing tools to construct the diagram so it is easier to modify in the future.
- Use a block arrow to indicate the direction of the relationship and fill it with a contrasting color so the direction is clear to the audience.
- Use different colors or shapes to represent the causes or outcomes if that will make the interpretation easier.

- To increase the visual impact, use photographs to fill the shapes for the cause or outcome so that the audience identifies more with each item.

To show mathematical relationships, use an Equation Diagram

A mathematical relationship does not need to involve numbers, it involves the function of adding or subtracting to get a result. It can be adding factors to arrive at a conclusion or subtracting certain features to arrive at a simpler product that can reach a lower price point in the marketplace. Here is an example of an equation diagram used instead of a text slide.

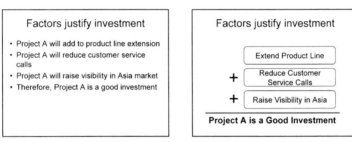

When creating an Equation Diagram, keep the following best practices in mind:

- Vertical equations are usually easier to understand because it is the first type of equation we learn in school (horizontally-oriented equations come in later grades).
- By positioning the text inside a shape, it separates the idea the text represents from the mathematical sign, making it easier to understand.
- Always include the "equals" line at the bottom before you state the conclusion so the audience knows where the equation ends.

- You can use a different color for the concluding statement to make it stand out more to the viewer.
- Use the software's drawing tools rather than a graphic program to construct the diagram so it is easier to modify in the future.

To Organize/Compare Ideas

Most comparisons are done by listing bullet points of text. This makes it hard for the audience to follow. A T-chart or matrix diagram arranges the information visually in an easier-to-understand manner. If you are comparing the same information at two points in time, a side-by-side arrangement of graphs or diagrams can make the point clearer. This section shows how to create diagrams that compare two or more items on one or more dimensions.

To show the comparison of items, use a T-Chart or Matrix Diagram

If you are talking about how two or more items compare on a number of criteria, a T-chart or matrix diagram is a good way to illustrate the comparison. Here is an example of a matrix diagram used instead of a text list.

Text Slide   *Visual*

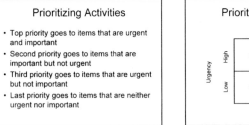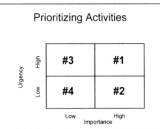

Here is an example of a T-chart used instead of a text list.

Text Slide   *Visual*

Plant Comparison
• Plant A is 15 years old, plant B is 30 years old
• Plant B is close to a rail line, plant A is not
• Plant A is close to highways, plant B is not
• Plant B has newer machinery than plant A
• Plant A is closer to the new residential areas than plant B

Plant Comparison

Plant A	Plant B
15 years old	30 years old
Far from rail line	Close to rail line
Close to highways	Far from highways
Older machinery	Newer machinery
Close to new housing	Farther from housing

When creating a T-chart or matrix diagram, keep the following best practices in mind:

- Use the software's drawing tools to create the diagram instead of a separate graphics program so that it is easier to change in the future.
- Increase the line thickness of each line to at least three points so the line is easy to see.
- To add text inside a square or a chart, create a separate text box and drag it on to the diagram to give yourself more formatting options for the text.
- Set the font size of any text large enough so that it can be seen as easily as text on any other slide.
- Make sure you clearly label the axis in a matrix diagram or the columns in a T-chart so that they are easily understood.

To show a comparison of the same item at two points in time, use Side-by-Side Graphs or Diagrams

You will often want to show how a measurement has changed from a previous point in time. Instead of putting the visuals that represent that measurement on individual slides, put them side-by-side so that the comparison is immediate and you do not have to flip back and forth between slides. Here is an example of a side-by-side comparison slide.

When creating side-by-side slides, keep the following best practices in mind:

- Make each graph or diagram the same size so that any changes are not exaggerated.
- Make sure each graph or diagram is created using the best practices described in other sections.
- Keep the parameters the same in each graph or diagram so you are showing a valid comparison, not comparing apples to oranges.
- Label each graph or diagram to indicate what time period or snapshot in time it represents.

To Share a Story or Example

Examples are a powerful way to prove the point we are making. Sometimes referred to as stories, they can be enhanced by adding a visual such as a photo, audio clip or video. A testimonial is another form of a story that can be enhanced by similar visuals. This section shows how to enhance a story or example with a photo, audio clip or video.

To enhance a story or example with a Picture

You have heard the saying that, "a picture is worth a thousand words." When you are sharing an example, this is especially true. Here is an example of using a picture instead of using a descriptive list.

Text Slide   *Visual*

Smithville Plant	Smithville Plant

- In top 20% of all plants on energy efficiency measures
- Productivity is in top quartile of comparable plants
- Located within 60 miles of three of our top six customers

Efficient, Productive, Close to customers

When using a picture on a slide, keep the following best practices in mind:

- If you are scanning a printed photo, make sure it is scanned at a resolution that is not too low so that the photo looks fuzzy when used and not too high so that the photo makes the slide file too large. For a 4" x 6" photo, 200 dots per inch (d.p.i.) is usually an adequate scanning resolution to use, with higher resolution needed for smaller pictures and lower resolution needed for larger pictures. Always save the scanned picture in a JPG file format for the best balance of file size and picture quality (JPG is also the preferred format for inserting into most software).

- If you are using a digital photo that you have taken or has been supplied to you, make sure you clean up and crop the photo before using it. By cleaning up, I refer to fixing any lighting issues, color issues and red eye with pictures of people. Crop the photo to eliminate any distracting or unnecessary backgrounds seen in the original photo. Always save the fixed photo to a new file name so that the original photo is not lost.

- After cleaning up and cropping a digital photo, you should also resample the photo down to an appropriate resolution. Most digital cameras have much higher resolution than a projector could ever use and the extra pixels make the slide file larger and run more slowly than it needs to. For example, a four megapixel photo has almost five times the number of pixels than a regular computer screen or projector could use. Resample photos down to XGA resolution (1024 x 768) so that it can be shown as a full screen graphic, if necessary, since most screens and projectors run at the XGA resolution. After you have used a graphics program to resample the photo, always save it to a new file name so that the original file is not lost.

- When you are inserting a photo onto a slide, always use the "Insert" feature instead of copying and pasting the picture from a viewer application. This is a safer method for inserting photos and will give you a more consistent high quality presentation.

- After you have inserted the photo on the slide, size it using the sizing handles to make it as large as you need it to be. Move it to the preferred position by grabbing it and dragging it to the correct location. Finally, if any touch-up cropping is required, use the cropping tool to make the final changes.

- Be very careful about using photos that come from the Internet. Copyright issues abound. All photos are copyrighted by the photographer or the company that hired the photographer to take the photo. You cannot just find a picture on the Internet and copy it into your presentation because, in almost all cases, you would be violating the copyright protection of the photo. Find sites that offer photos that you can download and use with permission of the owner of the picture. Make sure to read the permission statement to ensure that your usage is allowed. You can also purchase photos from stock photography sites that allow you to use the photo in certain usages, based on the type of license you purchase. See the Appendix for some online sources of photos.

To enhance a story or example with an Audio clip or Text

If you are quoting someone, you can use an audio clip of them saying the quote or print the quote on the slide for the audience to read. Here is an example of a quotation on a slide:

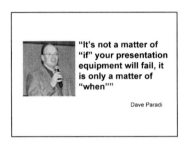

When you are using audio clips or quotations, keep the following best practices in mind:

- It is usually a good idea to put a picture of the speaker on the slide with the quotation or audio clip so that the audience is also using their visual pathway to absorb the message. Position the photo so that the person is facing the quotation because the audience will look where the person in the picture is looking.
- The quotation should be in larger type than the name of the person. In addition to the name of the person, you can also include the date, location, company or other information that would be relevant to the audience's interpretation or lend credibility to the quotation.
- When using an audio clip, make sure that the quality is high because any distortions will be magnified when the clip is played through a sound system.

- Adjust the volume of the audio clip or the output of your computer before you start presenting so that when the clip plays during the presentation, it is loud enough for everyone to hear. Remember that once you have everyone in the room, the ambient noise will be louder than it is when no one is there. So set the volume level in an empty room slightly louder than you need so that it sounds fine when everyone is there.

- The preferred audio clip file format is usually MP3 because it is a universal format that works well in any slide software.

- The preferred way of playing an audio clip is to incorporate it as part of a slide. This is better than exiting the slide software to play the clip in a media player application or creating a hyperlink to the audio file which will open the media player application. Incorporating the audio clip as part of the slide provides a seamless experience for the audience.

- Use the options in your slide software to control how and when the clip plays on a slide and whether you want the audience to see any controls as it plays. The best approach is usually to hide the controls to keep the slide clean and to eliminate any visual distractions that sometimes occur with media player software.

- An audio clip should be short, perhaps no longer than forty-five seconds, in order to keep the audience's attention when there is only a stationary visual image.

- When using an audio clip, make sure you introduce it properly. Let the audience know when you want them to pay particular attention and what they should be specifically listening for.

To include a Video when sharing a story or example

A video can be used to give visual context. It can show movement that demonstrates what you are sharing. It can even show how a computer application is used to perform a particular function.

Here is an example of a video used instead of a text list:

Text Slide   *Visual*

Gas valve safety

- Locate gas valve
- Inspect for damage or rust
- Determine open and closed positions
- Turn fully to closed
- Check that gas does not flow
- Begin maintenance service

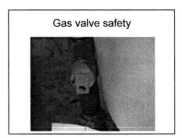

Gas valve safety

When you are using video clips, keep the following best practices in mind:

- Choose a video with as much resolution as you can get. Usually 640 x 480 or greater will work well. This gives you the clearest picture possible when it is shown. Remember that any distortions that you see on your screen will be magnified when shown on a larger screen in the meeting room.

- Learn the preferred video file format for the slide software you are using. Playing video as part of your slide is more difficult when you do not use a file format that is easy for your slide software to accommodate.

- When incorporating a video, consider whether the slide needs a title or not. Often with a video, a title can be distracting. Since you will typically run the video in a size that fills the screen, the title would not be seen with the video.

- Most slide software will not embed your video file as part of the slide file due to size concerns (video files can be quite large). Instead, they link to the video file on your disk drive. Most of the time it is best to save the video files and slide file in the same folder so that the link is short and will work better if you have to move the files to another computer to present.

- Use the options in your slide software to control how and when the video plays on a slide and whether you want the audience to see any controls as it plays. Hiding the controls is usually the best approach. Keep the slide clean and eliminate any visual distractions that can occur when using media player software.

- Adjust the volume of the video or the output of your computer before you start presenting so when the video plays during the presentation, it will be loud enough for everyone to hear. Remember that once you have everyone in the room, the ambient noise will be louder than when no one is there. So, set the volume level in an empty room slightly louder than you need so that it sounds good when everyone is there.

- The preferred way of playing a video is to incorporate it as part of a slide. This is better than exiting the slide software to play the clip in a media player application or creating a hyperlink to the video file, which would then open the media player application. Incorporating the video clip as part of the slide provides a seamless experience for the audience.

- Make sure the video clip is no longer than two minutes or the audience will start to tire of watching it. A presentation should be more interactive than a video; the audience wants to hear you expand or explain the ideas shown in the video.

- When using a video, make sure you introduce it properly by letting the audience know what, in particular, they should be watching for on the video. For example, you might say, "In the video that I am about to play, around twenty seconds in, watch closely as she describes how employee morale is being affected by the biggest problem in the plant."

- Make sure to test your video prior to your presentation, as soon as your computer is hooked up to a projector. Sometimes the power of the video system in a laptop is not enough to run a video on both the laptop screen and the projector at the same time. If this is an issue, the video will just show up as a black square on the slide, instead of showing the motion of the video. The only possible solution to try is to update the video drivers for your computer. If that does not remedy the problem, you will have to consider whether you need to use a different computer when presenting. Always test it on that computer first to make sure it works.

Presenting Time Based Information

Time-based information lends itself to a visual approach, rather than the less effective way of listing dates, or bullets and paragraphs that contain dates that get lost amongst the rest of the text. This section will show how to use a Gantt chart or calendar visual to represent time-based information.

To show timelines,
use a Gantt Chart

A Gantt chart shows duration of tasks or events as well as the sequence of those events along a timeline. It is commonly used in project management as well as to represent a series of events over time. Here is an example of a Gantt chart used instead of a text slide.

Text Slide   *Visual*

History of Market Influences
• U.S. dominated demand in 1980's and early 1990's
• Emergence of Asia in 1993-1999
• Europe demand surged in late 90's
• Asia demand strong again starting in 2004

When creating Gantt charts, keep the following best practices in mind:

- Always have a time scale along the horizontal axis at the bottom of the slide so that the start time and durations of the bars are in context.

- Try to limit the number of rows of bars to six or fewer to keep the slide from being cluttered.

- If necessary, place equally-spaced faint vertical gridlines to make it easier for the audience to understand when an event starts and ends.

- While you can produce Gantt charts in project management software, the resulting charts are usually cluttered, complex and confusing. In most cases, it is better to create the Gantt chart using the slide software's drawing tools so it will be clean and easy to change.

- Label each row and leave enough space between the rows so that the audience can easily tell which bars are in which rows.

- Use filled bars instead of hollow rectangles because it is easier to see the size of each bar and interpret what it means.

- Fill all the bars with the same color and use a highlight color only if one bar is more important than the others. Do not create a rainbow of colors for the bars. That distracts the audience.

To show date based information,
use a Calendar

Instead of simply listing dates as text, you can show the dates on a calendar to make them stand out and be remembered. Here is an example of a calendar used instead of a text slide.

Text Slide   *Visual*

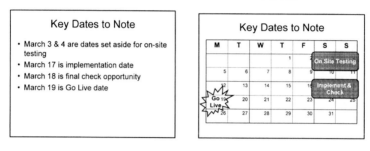

When creating calendars, keep the following best practices in mind:

- If the dates stretch across more than five weeks, split the slide into two slides, with one month on each. Otherwise, it will get too crowded to easily see what the dates are on a single calendar.
- Keep the highlighted dates to a maximum of four dates so that each stands out on its own.
- To highlight dates, use a shape that can cover the date range. This allows you to set a background color that provides contrast with the rest of the calendar background.
- Include the days of the week on the calendar to give the audience proper context. People relate much better to days of the week than they do to the numeric day during the month.

- Use the drawing tools or table feature of the slide software to create the calendar instead of using an image of a calendar because it will be easier to change in the future.
- Another option for highlighting just a single date range is to shade out all of the other dates so that only the single date range is clearly visible.

To Show Geographic Based Information, Use a Map

When you are presenting geographically-based data, such as sales in each region or inventory at each regional warehouse, show the data on a map. It gives the audience a much better understanding of the context than text. Here is an example of a map used instead of a table of numbers on a slide.

Text Slide   *Visual*

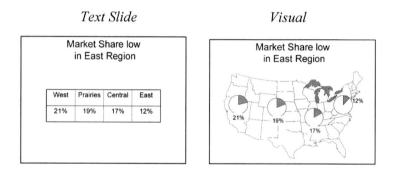

When creating maps, keep the following best practices in mind:

- Use the maps that you can find in the clip art section of your slide program or purchase a line art map of the area you want to show instead of scanning a map or drawing your own. A line art map will be much crisper and look better when projected.

- If you are using a map from clip art or one that you have purchased, read the license agreement to make sure you can use it in the presentation. Some maps have restrictions on how they can be used, so you need to be careful.

- Try to eliminate any background graphics or unneeded parts of the map so the focus is only on the area you want the audience to pay attention to.
- In addition to text, add graphics, such as graphs, on top of the map to place the data in a geographically visual context.
- You may need to add a solid color background to text boxes so that the text will show up on the map, since there can be many lines or other elements from the map that will show through a transparent background of a text box.

Highlighting Computer-Based Information

Information that is contained in other software programs sometimes needs to be shown in your presentation. Instead of annoying the audience by dropping out of the slide show and switching to another application, incorporate the information onto a slide. This section will cover how to include a screen capture from a website, link to a file that opens in another program automatically, and incorporate parts of a PDF file as a graphic on a slide.

To show what is on a computer screen, use a Screen Capture

With more information emanating from websites, it is only natural that you would want to incorporate some in your presentation. Some presenters have even tried to use live web links. This is risky, though, as live web links can be unreliable and tough to test beforehand. Instead, use a screen capture that will show the audience what you want them to see. Since this is a static part of your slide, it will not represent a risk when presenting. Here is an example of a slide with a screen capture on it.

When you are using screen captures, keep the following best practices in mind:

- Learn how to use the screen capture feature of your operating system or application to get the best quality capture.
- Size the window you are capturing to the largest size if you want the clearest capture possible. Keep in mind that you may want to keep the window smaller if you only want to show what a typical user would see on their screen.
- Use the cropping tool in your slide software to remove any parts of the screen capture that you will not need. Any extra graphics or text will distract from your point.
- Include the web page URL as a separate text box on the slide so that if someone wants to go to review that page later, they do not have to search for it.
- Screen captures also work for showing information out of other programs that are not web-based.

To link to another application file,
use a Hyperlink

There will be times when you will want to switch to a different application in the middle of your presentation. Perhaps you want to open up a word processor to capture audience comments for distribution after the meeting or you want to get input on some figures for a financial model. Instead of dropping out of the presentation and having the audience see you switch to the other application, use a hyperlink on a slide. Here is an example of a slide with a hyperlink on it.

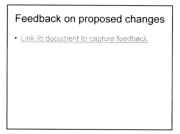

When using a hyperlink, keep the following best practices in mind:

- Most slide software programs allow you to create a hyperlink from either text or a graphic. Select which would be most appropriate in your presentation.
- Learn how to activate the hyperlink during your presentation. Most slide software programs have ways to activate hyperlinks using keyboard shortcuts instead of distracting the audience by moving the mouse cursor across the screen to click on the link.

- Check how to return to your presentation when you are finished in the other program. Most of the time it is as simple as exiting the other application. Make sure you save any changes or work you did in the other program before returning to your presentation.

To incorporate content in a PDF file,
use the PDF Snapshot Tool

Since more and more formerly paper documents are now being created as Adobe PDF documents, you may find it necessary to capture content from a PDF file. PDF files have an advantage over other types of files, since they look the same on different computing platforms and can contain high resolution graphics. This makes them ideal for capturing logos or other complex graphics. Fortunately, the Acrobat Reader software (which is freely downloadable from the Adobe website) makes this easy. After you open a PDF document, click on the snapshot tool (it looks like a camera and is usually found on the basic toolbar). Your cursor will turn into a crosshairs cursor that you can use to draw a rectangle around the content you want to copy. In your slide software, you can now paste what you had captured with the snapshot tool.

Keep these best practices in mind when using the Adobe snapshot tool:

- Size your Acrobat window as large as you can and zoom in on the item you want to capture so that the item fills as much of the window as possible. This will result in the highest resolution capture and give you more flexibility when using the pasted image in your slide software.

- In your slide software, the pasted item will be an image. Use the image tools, such as cropping and sizing tools, to get the pasted image to look exactly the way you want it to.

- Using the snapshot tool will yield better results than using a simple screen capture of the Adobe Acrobat window.

By using the best practices for creating the visuals listed above, your slides should now be well on their way to being the persuasive visuals that you need to present confidently to decision-makers. The next chapter will look at how to make the visuals you have created even clearer and more powerful.

Slide Makeover Examples

Example #1: Sales Presentation Slide

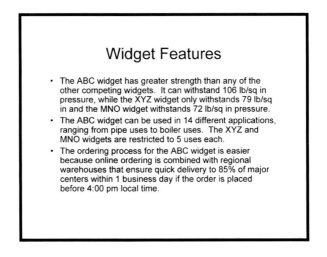

In the previous chapter we decided that a column graph would be the best way to show the strength advantage that the ABC widget has over the competition. Here is the slide with the new headline and column graph:

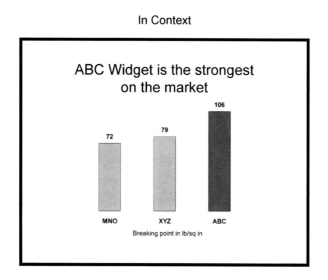

We have followed the best practices for creating column graphs and the point is now clear in a visual way.

Example #2: Current Situation Presentation Slide

Project Status

Phase	Budget ('000s)		Schedule	
	Actual	Planned	Actual	Planned
Design	185	172	Jun-27	Jun-15
Development	27	156		Nov-18
Testing	0	97		Feb-02
Implementation	0	124		Apr-30

Notes on Progress:
- Phase 1 finished a few days late and cost overrun was due to extra shipping costs of parts from supplier
- Phase 2 progress a little slow due to more complex design decided on in Phase 1
- May run in to cost and schedule challenges if design is too complex to integrate into existing processes and equipment
- Still working on buy-in on selected design

When we last looked at this slide, we decided to create a process diagram of the future state that would show the critical buy-in issues that needed to be addressed. Here is the slide with the new headline and process diagram.

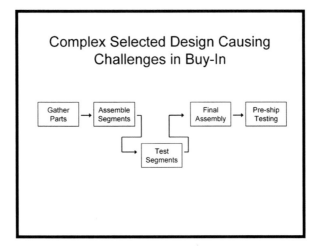

The process diagram shows the steps and the flow clearly. The new step of testing segments is shown as the additional step that is inserted into the process.

CHAPTER SIX

Crystal Clear

Your slides now have properly developed headlines and visuals instead of bullet points, but we are not yet finished with the visuals. A visual is more intuitively understood than a list of bullet points, but if the audience is not able to determine the most important part of the visual, they may take away a different message than you intended. In order to guarantee that they get the right message as vividly as possible, this chapter will show you how to enhance the clarity of the visuals you have created. We will discuss adding callouts and other techniques to enhance the appearance of different elements of the visuals.

Callouts to Direct Audience Attention

A callout directs the decision-maker's attention to the most important part of the visual. Callouts eliminate the need for the presenter to use a pointing device or laser pointer to try to point out important areas on a visual. When a presenter uses a pointing device or walks to the screen and points at parts of the screen, it is distracting and ineffective for a number of reasons.

If you use a laser pointer, it is very hard to hold the laser dot in one spot without it moving. This results in the dot jiggling on the screen. Our eyes are always drawn to movement, so the wiggling dot will attract the attention and the audience will pay less attention to what you are saying. Most laser pointers are red. This can be a problem for up to 11% of the male Caucasian population that has some degree of red-green color blindness because they may not see it at all.

If you walk to the screen and point with a stick or your arm, you almost always end up walking in front of the projected image, blocking some of the visual and reducing the context for the audience. Depending on how the screen is set up and where the image is on the screen, you may be unable to physically reach the intended spot on the screen and you end up pointing to a different spot while trying to get the audience to look elsewhere on the slide. Both methods result in more audience confusion and less clarity of your message.

There are two parts to any callout—the graphic highlight and the callout text. The graphic highlight is a graphic used to indicate the most important part of the visual. The purpose is to direct the audience's attention to that specific spot. It may be an arrow, line, square, oval or other shape. The callout text is the text that explains what the graphic highlight is pointing out so that the audience knows why you are highlighting that spot in the visual. A callout needs to serve both purposes—directing attention and explaining why the attention is being directed to that spot. Too often, callouts consist of only one of these two elements.

Example of callout with graphic highlight and callout text

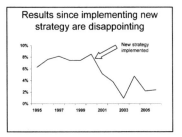

Examples of Graphic Highlights

The first element of a callout is the graphic highlight. Depending on what you want to highlight on the visual, you could use an arrow graphic to point to a spot or a shape graphic to focus attention on an area. Below are some examples of types of arrows and shapes that can be used as graphic highlights.

Graphic arrow

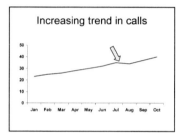

Regular arrow

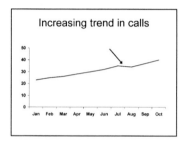

Circle/Oval

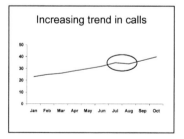

Rounded/Regular Rectangle

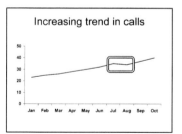

Best Practices for Creating Graphic Highlights

The greatest challenge when creating a graphic highlight is selecting a color for the highlight that will have enough contrast with the underlying colors of the slide or the parts of the visual. This can often be difficult because the colors of a visual will contrast with the slide background; finding another color that contrasts with both is very hard. Here are some best practices for creating graphic highlights:

- If you can find a single color to use for a graphic highlight, ensure that the highlight is thick enough to be easily seen. A minimum thickness of three points is usually a good guideline to use.
- If there are multiple colors that will be behind the graphic highlight, use a combination of colors to ensure contrast in all areas. A technique that works well is to use or create a graphic highlight that has a thick black outline and a bright yellow interior. This ensures that in dark background areas the bright yellow is easily seen and in light background areas the black is visible. Here are two examples:

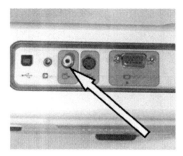
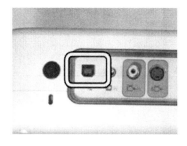

If your slide software does not allow you to create a shape that has two colors in the outline, you can create your own shape. The rounded rectangle shown in the example above is actually created from two rounded rectangles. The first rectangle was drawn with no fill color and a thick (9 point) black outline. This rectangle was then copied and pasted. The second rectangle was set to have a bright yellow thinner (4.5 point) outline. The second rectangle was then moved on top of the first rectangle, making it appear that a single rectangle has two contrasting colors as the outline. This technique of contrasting colors will allow a graphic callout to be seen in every situation.

- Try to position the callout so that it does not cover up too much of the underlying visual. If too much of the visual is obscured, the audience will lose context. For lines or arrows, extend them so that the tail is far enough away that the text you add will not cover up much of the visual. For shapes such as ovals or rectangles, you may need to add a line that extends away from the visual to connect the relevant text to the shape (as shown in the example on page 106). If the shape must cover up a part of the visual, consider using a semi-transparent fill color for the shape so that the underlying visual can be partially seen.

Best Practices for Callout Text

Just as the graphic highlight needs to be seen when positioned on the visual, so the audience must be able to see the text as well. Here are some best practices when creating the callout text:

- Use a separate text box for the callout text instead of using an existing text box or placeholder. This allows you to format and position the text exactly where you want it to be. Size the text box to contain the text and little else so that it is compact and not overly large. Set the fill color of the text box to be transparent so that any portion of the visual that happens to be under the text box will show through.

- Choose a font that is at least twenty point or larger so that the text is easily read when projected or printed in handout form.

- If the text must be placed on top of the visual, you may have the challenge of finding a text color that will contrast with the variety of colors in the visual underneath the text. The best solution is to fill the text box with a contrasting color so that the text is easily seen, but make the fill semi-transparent so that the audience can still faintly see the underlying visual. This allows the text to be read while still maintaining the context of the visual underneath.

Example of text with semi-transparent background and line connecting graphic highlight to callout text

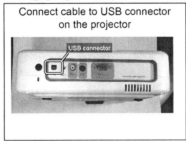

Improving the appearance of visual elements

Many slide software programs allow you to fill shapes, including those used in graphs, with special fill effects or even pictures. These techniques allow you to bring the context of the slide out even further and make the message clearer. While you will not want to do this every time, it can add meaning to certain visuals.

Here is an example of a visual that has pictures added:

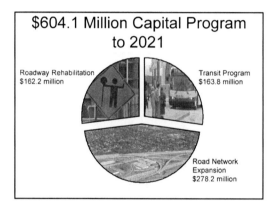

You can also use gradient fills to make a shape or bars or columns in a graph look more appealing. Here is an example of a gradient fill used on shapes in a diagram:

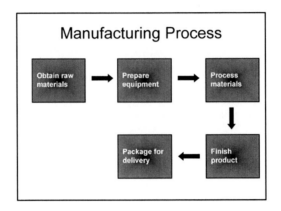

Other emphasis techniques that can be used to draw attention to a certain element of a visual include effects such as glow or shadow, which serve to make a shape stand out from other similar shapes in the visual. These special effects could be useful when focusing attention on one step in a process or one bar in a graph.

When you are deciding on whether or not to use a special graphical fill for a shape or part of a graph, keep in mind that these techniques should only be used if they will add to the audience's understanding of the visual and not distract from it. Many slide software packages now include features that will allow you to change the graphic look of many of the elements of a visual, but too many of the effects they include only serve to distract the attention of the decision-maker. Keep any enhancements focused on making the visual more meaningful.

De-emphasizing elements to give context

Another way to emphasize a certain section of a visual is to partially cover up the rest of the visual so that the only section left clearly visible is the one you want the audience to focus on. Here is an example of one cell in a table being emphasized by covering up the other parts of the table:

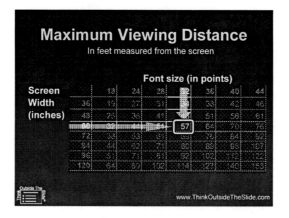

It is important that the audience can still see the rest of the visual so they have context, but, by covering up most of it, you make the visual less confusing and focus attention where you want it to be. To create this type of emphatic effect, draw shapes to cover up the parts of the visual that you want to de-emphasize. Set the fill color of the shape to be a similar shade to the slide background color and make the fill semi-transparent so that the underlying visual can still be seen through. You may need to create more than one shape to cover up all the parts of the visual (the above example used three semi-transparent rectangles to accomplish the effect).

Slide Makeover Examples

Example #1: Sales Presentation Slide

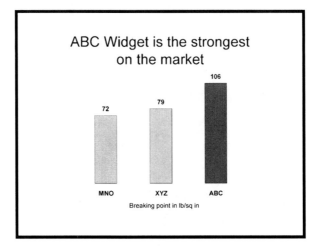

In the previous chapter, we created the column graph that replaced a paragraph of text. To accentuate the point that the ABC widget was the strongest, we added a callout that shows the strength advantage on the graph and emphasizes the magnitude of the advantage with text. Here is the slide with the callout added.

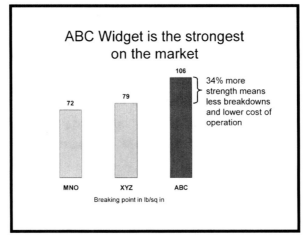

The key point of the strength advantage has been illustrated with a visual and is now further enhanced with a callout that drives home the benefit of this advantage.

Example #2: Current Situation Presentation Slide

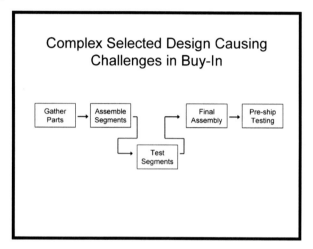

We last left this slide with a process diagram instead of the chart of numbers and text, but adding a callout will help even further. Here is the slide with the callout added to the process diagram.

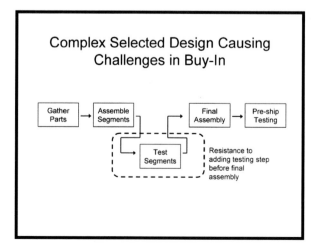

The callout draws the decision-maker's attention to the new step of testing each segment before final assembly. This is where the project is running into resistance and the graphic makes it crystal clear to the decision-makers. They will now know where they need to focus their efforts in resolving this issue.

CHAPTER SEVEN

Keep Focus

The first four steps of the KWICK method have focused on creating the visual slides. This fifth step centers on how you present that visual slide for maximum impact. It is a big step forward to use visual slides instead of bullet-point slides, but it is even better when you control those visuals in a way that helps you persuade the decision-makers more effectively. This chapter will cover building the slides with animation, breaking down complex visuals and employing some advanced techniques for using visuals.

Building the Visual with Animation

If you display the visual slide all at once, the audience may not know where to look first. It also does not give you an opportunity to set the right context or lay foundation concepts before other ideas. By building the elements of the visual on the slide, you have the opportunity to speak to each part of the visual and give it the proper attention it deserves.

For example, when you are speaking about a column graph, you will likely want to build each column one at a time so that you can speak about the meaning of that column. In a process diagram, you would build each step in the process to be able to explain that step and how it fits in to the overall point you are making.

One way to create the building of elements on a slide is to create multiple slides, each with one more element added to the overall visual. While this works, it is usually more time-consuming to create and harder to work with when you want to make changes, because you have to change multiple slides. An easier way to build elements on a slide is to use the animation feature of your slide software. This feature allows you to select any element on the slide and give instructions on when and how that element should appear on the slide.

While I am suggesting you use the animation feature to build the points on your slides, why is it that so much of the animation we see annoys us? This result occurs because the presenter went for entertainment value instead of remembering that the focus should be on the clarity of understanding. Most slide software programs include fancy animation effects that enable you to make an element fly, twirl or bounce on the slide. Too often, presenters get seduced by these "cool" effects and include them in their presentations. The unfortunate result is that these "cool" effects actually annoy the audience and decision-makers are distracted. They will tune out quickly if they perceive an "amateur" quality to the presentation. Save the fancy effects for your uncle's birthday party slideshow.

When using the animation feature of your slide software, here are some best practices to keep in mind:

- To avoid annoying the audience, use simple animation effects only. Suggestions include:
  - Making text simply appear instead of moving across the slide,
  - Using movement of an arrow or line towards the spot you want the audience to focus on, and
  - Revealing a picture using a fade-in technique to add the element of surprise to what the picture shows.

- Sequence the elements in the correct order so that you can logically build the visual with your explanation.

- Always test the animations and the sequence before you deliver your presentation to make sure that your message is logically supported by the visual.

- Some slide software programs also offer the option of removing an element from the slide, using animation as you present. This could be useful if you want to show an existing situation first. Then, remove an element or two that illustrates some changes that are being proposed. This gives the visual more context because the audience sees the starting point and what changes to get to the ending situation.

- Sometimes your software will not allow you to build the elements in the order or manner that you would like. One option, if your software allows it, is to use the feature to remove an element from the slide. You create the illusion of a part of the visual appearing by removing a shape that is covering up that part of the visual.

- Do not use the automatic timing or pre-set animation features if your software contains these features. Having movement or building pre-sets by the software reduces the control you have over your presentation and can cause difficulties when presenting.

- One reason some presenters avoid building elements on their slides is that they do not want to be stuck standing next to their computer since each build requires you to press a key on the computer to make the build happen on the slide. Purchase and use a presentation remote that allows you to stand away from the computer and remotely advance the next build on the slide. Many remotes are widely available and will give you much more freedom in delivering your next presentation.

Breaking down complex visuals

One challenge with using visuals is that they can sometimes get quite complex. Even building elements of a complex visual may not save you from ending up with the audience confused, due to the complexity of what is being presented. The best solution is to use the Break-Down & Zoom-In technique.

The Break-Down & Zoom-In technique is consistent with our desire to give context to the audience. It works in the following way:

1. First, you show the slide that has the entire visual on it. Explain that you are showing this slide only to give the overall context. Use semi-transparent shapes to indicate the different parts that you want to discuss. This puts the audience at ease that they are not about to be overloaded with complexity on a single slide.

2. Move to the next slide which has a zoomed-in view of the whole visual, showing only the first part you want to discuss. Now you can build this smaller section of the overall visual and keep the explanation limited to the section that you are focused on.

3. Go back to the overall visual briefly to show where you have just been and where you are headed next. This keeps the audience following along because they understand how each piece fits in to the overall picture.

4. Alternate between zoomed in slides and the overall visual until each part has been explained. End with the overall visual to tie all the pieces together.

This technique can be used for diagrams that are complex, imported graphics or pictures. In each case, you can show the overall visual to give context and keep context by alternating between zoomed-in details and the overall visual.

In one situation, I used the break-down and zoom-in technique to make an imported document easier to understand. It was a balance sheet that the presenter needed to explain, but shown as a whole, the text would be too small. So I added semi-transparent boxes over the entire balance sheet to break it down into sections. Then, for each section, a slide was created with only that section enlarged to clearly show the content that needed to be explained.

Non-linear presentations

Our premise throughout this book has been that your presentation must remain focused on the audience and their needs. What if you could ask the audience what they want to hear about and be able to immediately deliver that content? It would make every presentation instantly customized and would certainly allow you to stand out from the rest of the presenters the decision-makers will see. It would allow you to use the visual slides that are best suited for that group at that time. This type of presentation is what I call a non-linear presentation.

A traditional slide presentation proceeds from the first slide to the last slide in the file in a linear manner. The audience has to sit through the slides in the order the presenter chose regardless of whether that is the order the audience would have chosen. A non-linear presentation presents the audience with a menu of items that the presenter can talk about and the audience decides which topics will be covered and in what order. The presenter may give the presentation to different audiences and the topics and sequence will vary each time.

In a sales situation, a non-linear presentation would introduce the proposal and then ask the audience which aspect of the proposal they wanted to discuss first. The presenter moves to the highest-priority module based on audience feedback and goes through the visual slides for that topic. When done, the presenter returns to the menu of topics. The next most important aspect of the proposal is selected and the cycle is repeated until the decision-makers have the information they need to be able to proceed with a decision. You may end up going through all of the modules or very few, but the audience gets exactly what they need at that moment.

It is possible that some audience members will feel frustrated if their high-priority topics do not get chosen. In practice, you should make sure to cover enough of the topics to ensure everyone has at least a few of their priority topics covered. In a sales situation, let the key decision-maker drive the selection of topics because they are the most influential person in the audience.

When designing a non-linear presentation, you must think in terms of modules of information. Each module covers a specific topic and can be presented on its own. This allows any sub-set of these modules to be used in a certain presentation. The audience sees the menu of modules and decides which modules they are interested in and in what order.

Illustration of a non-linear presentation

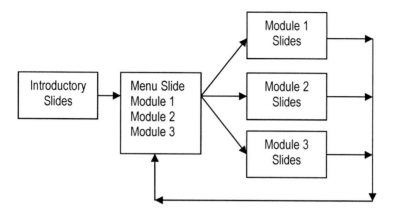

If you want the presentation to look completely seamless, you can design each module with the same slide introducing the module, like a module title slide, and a common module end slide, such as a module summary slide. This makes the audience see a smooth flow from one module to the next throughout the entire presentation.

A non-linear presentation should not be attempted by beginning presenters or by those not familiar with every topic in the presentation. A non-linear presentation requires the presenter to have detailed knowledge of every section of the presentation and to be comfortable switching between sections that may not be in the order they expected. It requires more preparation, but experts in a topic should be able to use this technique without much effort.

To create a non-linear presentation, check your slide software program for features that allow you to move between slides in an order you determine, not necessarily the order that the slides are found in the file. Sometimes a program will allow you to specify the slide number to jump to, sometimes it will allow hyperlinks to connect to a specific slide and sometimes you can set up your presentation to call other presentation files that contain each module. Learn how your software allows non-linear switching between slides and test it so that you are comfortable with how it works.

As you gain more experience presenting, consider if a non-linear presentation could allow you to reach a group of decision-makers in a way that would make them sit up and take notice.

Web based presentations

Increasingly, presenters are asked to use web-based presentation tools to deliver their presentation without the audience in the same room. This is due to audience members being geographically dispersed and the high travel costs to bring them all together for what may be a relatively short presentation when compared to the travel time. Web-based presentations also occur when meetings are called on short notice and there is literally no time for the audience to travel to a common site to see the presentation.

Web conferencing tools connect each audience member through the browser application on their computer to a central service. You connect as the presenter to the service and your presentation is then "pushed" out to each audience member, who sees it in their browser window. You are connected to the audience by a phone conference service for the audio part of the presentation.

While web presentations are rapidly becoming more popular due to the cost savings associated with travel, they do present a challenge for presenters. As a presenter, you can no longer rely on non-verbal feedback to determine the audience's reaction to your message. It does place a greater emphasis on clear visuals with callouts since the audience cannot see you "point" to something on the screen.

Some best practices to keep in mind when delivering a web presentation:

- No matter how fast your Internet connection, or how fast the connections of your audience members are, there will be a delay between when you ask your next slide or item to be displayed on their screen and when it actually gets displayed. This is due to bandwidth delays in the system and it can vary by time or geographic location. There is nothing you can do to decrease it or eliminate it. One way you can better synchronize what you are saying with what the audience is seeing is to set up a second computer on your desk and connect it to the conference as a participant. Position the screen of the participant computer so you can see it as they will be seeing it. After you "push" an item out to the web conference service, keep speaking about how the current topic ties to the next topic until you see the new idea appear on your participant screen. This is not perfect, but it gives you the best estimate of when the audience has been updated with your new information on their screen.

- Most web conferencing services have you share your screen in the web conferencing system to deliver your presentation. In this method, the web conferencing system constantly takes pictures of your screen and transmits those pictures to your audience. This allows you to use other content such as hyperlinked content from other applications since the audience will see exactly what you see.

- Because of the bandwidth delays already mentioned, you should eliminate any animation effects that have movement. They will appear choppy and disjointed if they work at all when viewed by the audience. Use the simple animation effect of making the element appear in place instead.

- Recognize that audience members will be multitasking because you cannot see what they are doing. One feature of many web conferencing systems is the ability to set up audience polls during the presentation. At an appropriate time in the presentation, you can ask everyone to answer a quick one or two question poll, usually located on the side of the web conferencing system screen. The responses are shown immediately and you can adjust your presentation to the responses in real time.

- Most audio conferencing systems offer you the option to mute all attendees or allow an open line where everyone can hear what everyone else is saying at all times. If you have a relatively small group, up to fifteen to twenty audience members, you can use an open line to promote discussion and sharing of ideas. If you have a large audience, you will likely want to mute the group so that the background noise does not get too distracting. With either choice, you should always let the participants know how an individual audience member can mute just their line in case they are on a speaker phone or in a noisy environment such as a manufacturing facility or airport, because the background noise from the one phone can make it very hard for everyone to hear.

Slide Makeover Examples

Example #1: Sales Presentation Slide

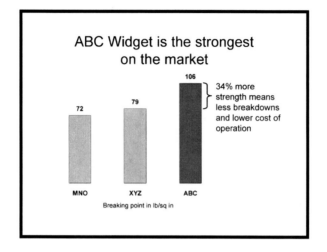

The only thing left to add to our visual slide from the last chapter is to decide how to build the elements on the slide. Here is how I would suggest sequencing the builds for the visual:

1. Show the columns for the competing products. Explain why strength is important in a widget.
2. Show the column for the ABC widget. Point out how it clearly outpaces the competition.
3. Show the callout. Reinforce the advantage of widget strength in their facility.

By sequencing the parts of the visual, we can build the key point that the ABC widget's strength advantage is of great benefit to these decision makers.

Example #2: Current Situation Presentation Slide

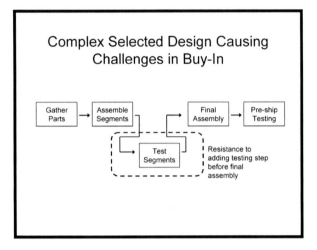

The build sequence for this slide is a little more complex because I would suggest that it include use of a previous slide. Here is what I recommend:

1. Display a slide that shows the current process that does not include the testing of segments. Explain that this is the current process in use.

2. Display the four existing process steps (Gather Parts, Assemble Segments, Final Assembly, and Pre-ship Testing). Explain how Phase One of the project has inserted a new step between Assemble Segments and Final Assembly (this will explain why there is a gap in the middle of the diagram).

3. Display the new step, Test Segments and the lines that tie it to the existing steps. You can then discuss why this is a good change based on the results of Phase One.

4. Display the callout to focus discussions on the reasons the new step is meeting resistance from the staff.

By sequencing the information and including a new slide prior to this slide to give better context, this visual will now focus the attention of the decision-makers on what they need to do in order to address this important issue.

CHAPTER EIGHT

Putting the KWICK Method into Practice

Will the KWICK method create a dramatic difference in the slides that you create? Let us review the "before" and "after" slides for the two examples we have been using throughout the book.

Slide Makeover Examples

Example #1: Sales Presentation Slide

Before   *After*

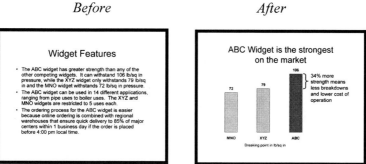

Quite a dramatic improvement! The KWICK method resulted in a persuasive visual that will have far more impact than the text-overloaded slide we started with.

Example #2: Current Situation Presentation Slide

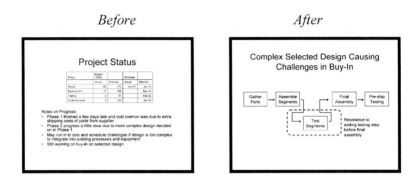

Before   *After*

Again, the KWICK method delivered a significant improvement in both clarity and the ability to influence decision-makers.

By now you understand that creating persuasive visuals for your presentation is not complicated—you just need to refocus your efforts and it will have positive results almost immediately. Instead of sitting down and typing out what you will say as bullet points on a slide, work through the KWICK method to create a more visually appealing and persuasive set of slides.

If it seems like too much effort to use the KWICK method on all of the slides in a large presentation, start small. Select the three to five most important slides in the presentation and work on those first. Then, build your skills and comfort level as you work on another few slides for the next time you present. Pretty soon, you will have worked through all of the slides and your presentation will be transformed. To see how much it has changed, go back to the first version and compare. You will be amazed at the difference.

Leverage your work with a Slide Library

Now that you have used the KWICK method to create powerful visuals to use during your presentations, leverage the investment you have made. The next time you have to create a presentation, re-use the great visuals you have created that apply to the new situation and create slides for the new ideas you will be sharing.

One problem remains, though. After you have done this a number of times, how do you know where to find the slide you are looking for? You know it may be in one of the presentations you did recently, but which one?

You can save hours of searching and frustration by creating and maintaining a slide library. I define a slide library as a single slide file that contains the key slides that you use on a regular basis. It is not intended to hold every slide you could ever use. Whether you do sales presentations, financial presentations or training workshops, there are certain core topics that you cover in almost every presentation. The visuals you have created for these core topics are the slides that should be in your slide library.

When you start work on a new presentation, you start with your analysis of the situation and the audience to determine which messages you need to include. Open up a new presentation in your slide software and copy the slides you need from the slide library. Then, all you have to do is arrange the slides in the right order and create new visuals for any of the topics not covered by the slides from the library. In many cases, the slide library will contain 70% or more of the slides you will use each time you present.

Set aside time every four months to review the slides in your library. Update them with the latest data or revise them with new ideas to make them more effective. Updating the library more frequently will likely become a burden and it will not get done at all. Less frequently and the slides in the library get too far out of date. The four month cycle is a guideline that may not fit every situation, but it usually strikes a balance between the work required and the currency of the information used on the slides.

Because your slide library is so valuable, ensure that it is backed up regularly. You would not want to lose it after putting all that work into it.

If you work with colleagues, look at creating a library that everyone can contribute to and access. Your presentations will become more consistent as a group and the effort of updating will be spread amongst a number of presenters, making it less burdensome for each one.

There are now technology solutions that maintain libraries of slides on a network system that can be accessed over the web and rules set up as to who can use or modify certain slides. If you have a number of people who should be using a slide library in multiple geographic locations, see if one of these solutions may be a good fit for your situation.

Build on your success

You have reached the end of the book and are now equipped to use the KWICK method to transform boring, text-overloaded slides into persuasive visuals. As you present these visual slides, watch the reaction of the decision-makers in your audience. You will hear positive comments and see how your presentations lead to better results. Build on those successes and you will have a starring role in The Visual Slide Revolution.

APPENDIX

In this appendix, I have listed numerous resources to use as you continue to learn and develop visual presentations. The resources have been divided up into the following sections:

- Resources for Visual Content
- Presentation Consulting and Design Resources
- Web sites and Blogs
- Book Recommendations
- Training Resources

Go to **www.VisualSlideRevolution.com** for details on the companion video training CD that shows you specific techniques in PowerPoint to implement the ideas in this book.

More details of my training and consulting services are in this section. If you want to contact me to discuss your specific training or presentation consulting needs:

Phone: **(905) 510-4911**
E-mail: **Dave@ThinkOutsideTheSlide.com**
Web: **www.ThinkOutsideTheSlide.com**

Resources for Visual Content

istockphoto.com – this stock photography web site contains over 1 million photos that have been selected from images submitted by mostly professional photographers. You can search for the image you want and the purchase price is usually under $5 for a resolution that will work well on a slide.

istockvideo.com – a companion site to istockphoto listed above, it contains a library of short video clips at reasonable prices that can be used in presentations. Most of the clips do not have sound, so you can add your own sound or audio.

www.billiondollargraphics.com – This site, by artist Michael Parkinson, contains ideas and products that help you design graphics. It is aimed at those who want to design more complex or higher end graphic images. See **www.billiondollargraphics.com/businessgraphiclibrary.html** for some sample ideas.

www.mapsfordesign.com – At this site you can purchase high quality editable line drawing maps that are ideal for slide usage. The maps are easy to separate when you want to extract only certain regions or states. The map shown in the example in chapter 5 is from this site.

www.plays2run.com – An innovative site that discusses ways to influence others based on real world research. As you explore each of the play types, pay attention to the ideas given and consider how you may create graphics that illustrate the point you are making. Use this as a site to stir your creativity.

www.pointclips.com – This site has some of the best looking clip art available. To call it clip art is actually to understate the quality of the vector art that you can find here. They sell packages of similar themed art that would look good on slides.

www.visual-literacy.org/periodic_table/periodic_table.html – The web site is a project from some academics who are studying ways to represent concepts visually. This page contains a large number of potential visual ideas organized into categories based on the periodic table of elements (there's the academic influence showing through). Notice that they have organized the visual methods (as they term them) by color to represent what you are trying to visualize (data, concept, strategy, etc.) and they have added letter colors and symbols to further categorize the methods on the basis of process vs. structure, detail vs. overview and divergent vs. convergent thinking. It may seem a little too academic, but roll your mouse over any of the boxes in the table, and you will see a popup example of the visual relating to that method. It is interesting to see some of the examples and it will give you ideas for your own visuals.

www.powerframeworks.com – A subscription site that has a large library of already created slides using visuals to represent concepts. You subscribe to the site and can then download any of the ready to use frameworks as they call them. A good site for ideas and ready made graphics for your presentations.

Presentation Consulting and Design Resources

The PowerPoint Presentation Effectiveness System

My research based PowerPoint Presentation Effectiveness System helps my clients achieve greater productivity and deliver presentations that sell ideas, products and services more effectively to decision makers.

A single training session, book or set of standard slides will not by itself solve the issues of effectiveness and efficiency that your team struggles with. These elements, along with others, need to be integrated in order to give you and your staff the maximum benefit. My approach is to work with you to identify the issues and provide solutions that bring lasting benefits in the future.

Steps my clients find most valuable:

Step 1: Identify common ideas your team communicates to others about products, services or operations

Step 2: Create a standard library of slides to visually communicate the common ideas

Step 3: Identify how your team will use the slides in the library to create a customized presentation

Step 4: Assess your team on their use of best practices and skills for creating and delivering effective PowerPoint presentations

Step 5: Create and deliver a customized training session

Step 6: Provide reference materials

Step 7: Follow-up Evaluation

Call me at **(905) 510-4911** to discuss how the **PowerPoint Presentation Effectiveness System** can start making a measurable difference in the presentations your team delivers.

Other Presentation Design Resources

Nancy Duarte and Duarte Design

Duarte Design is best known for the work they have done on the presentation that was turned into the Academy Award winning documentary "An Inconvenient Truth". When presenters want to hire the top presentation design firm around, Duarte Design is always on the short list. See their work and contact them at **www.duarte.com**.

Julie Terberg

One of the most respected presentation designers in the U.S., Julie works magic with the features of PowerPoint. Her animated slides make you swear you are watching a high end movie. Learn more at **www.terbergdesign.com**.

Echo Swinford

Based in Indianapolis, Echo is respected for her deep knowledge and talent at presentation design. If you need a makeover or a whole new design, check out her work at **www.echosvoice.com**. Echo is also one of the key contributors on the PowerPoint newsgroup.

Julie Marie Irvin

Julie and her Texas based team design presentations for a wide variety of clients. Check out their work on their site at **www.keystone-resources.com**.

Sandy Johnson

Another of the great PowerPoint MVPs who design and creates presentations from a base in Minnesota. Check out her work at **www.presentationwiz.biz**.

ProPoint Graphics

This NYC based group can help with a high end graphic look and Flash products. Their web site is **www.propointgraphics.com**.

Web sites and Blogs

ThinkOutsideTheSlide.com – My web site is the hub for more information on training workshops, consulting services and my books and videos. You can also read over 40 articles, more than 150 back issues of my newsletter and sign up for your own free subscription to the bi-weekly PowerPoint Tips newsletter.

Pptideas.blogspot.com – This blog contains my weekly insights and observations on the world of presenting with visuals. Read my latest thoughts and subscribe to the RSS feed.

Indezine.com – One of the most visited and respected sources of information on presenting with PowerPoint or Keynote.

SixMinutes.dlugan.com – This blog on public speaking and presentations does a weekly summary of interesting blog posts in the area of presenting and keeps a list of blogs that the writer finds useful (86 blogs at the time this is being written).

Book Recommendations

Made to Stick by Chip Heath & Dan Heath

ISBN 978-1-4000-6428-1 – available at all bookstores
(published by Random House)

Influence by Robert B. Cialdini

ISBN 978-0-06-124189-5 – available in bookstores (published
by Harper Collins)

Multimedia Learning by Richard E. Mayer

ISBN 0-521-78749-1 – can be ordered through a bookstore or
online book seller (published by Cambridge University Press)

Training Resources

Think Outside The Slide™ workshops

Want every member of your team to learn the KWICK method and see it applied to the slides you use today? Book a customized workshop that teaches the professionals and executives on your team how to transform their overloaded text slides into persuasive visuals. A half-day or full-day session incorporates detailed instruction along with "makeover" examples drawn from the slides you are using.

Call me at **(905) 510-4911** today to help your team create presentations that sell ideas, products and services more effectively to decision makers.

Books and Training Videos by Dave Paradi

The Visual Slide Revolution "How To" Video Training CD

You've been to PowerPoint training courses or have picked up most of your skills through trial and error. You are pretty good at using the software, except you don't know how to do some of the things shown in chapters five and six, like creating a semi-transparent fill for a shape or drawing a callout arrow that contains contrasting colors. You've just never been shown how to use some of the features of PowerPoint that would help you create the persuasive visuals that your presentations deserve. That's why there is **The Visual Slide Revolution "How To" Video Training CD**. This CD contains short video lessons that quickly show you how to create the elements of the visuals you want to create. See the full list of videos and get your copy today at **www.VisualSlideRevolution.com**.

Guide to PowerPoint

If you need a "how to" book that covers proper design principles and the essential skills to get started with PowerPoint 2003 or 2007, pick up a copy of "**Guide to PowerPoint**". Available at major bookstores or online at **www.ThinkOutsideTheSlide.com**, this slim reference guide keeps the key ideas at your fingertips. Don't waste your time on an "everything you ever and never wanted to know" 400+ page book. Pick up the concise guide that accelerates your learning curve and is the ideal desk reference.

In-depth videos

If you prefer to learn by watching a video, check out the **in-depth videos** available at **www.ThinkOutsideTheSlide.com**. In these videos, you see Dave present the best practices and then watch as he explains how to create the slides you just saw him present. Since you are watching the videos on your computer, you can pause at any time and switch over to your presentation to apply the ideas you are learning. Titles available include:

- Incorporating Video in Your PowerPoint Presentation
- Create a Custom Template
- Non-Linear and Advanced Delivery Techniques
- Creating Effective Graphs in PowerPoint Presentations
- Using Digital Photographs in PowerPoint Presentations
- Linking Excel Data to Your PowerPoint Slides
- Using Images
- Using Diagrams
- Setting up for a Worry Free Presentation
- Handling Problems During Your Presentation

Free online PowerPoint Effectiveness Assessment

How do you know if you follow best practices for creating effective PowerPoint presentations? How do you know if you have all the necessary skills for creating and delivering PowerPoint presentations that get results?

The answer is unfortunately, you don't know.

Now, for the first time, you can benchmark yourself against proven best practices and the skills needed to create and deliver effective PowerPoint presentations. I have taken my years of experience and created an online assessment that will check 40 best practices and 74 specific skills for effective PowerPoint presentations. Start benchmarking yourself today at **www.ThinkOutsideTheSlide.com/assessment.htm**. The assessment only takes 10-15 minutes to complete and then you receive a personalized report by e-mail listing the areas you are doing well in and those you need to work on. Using this report, you will be able to target your learning and improve your presentation ability quickly by focusing on those areas of greatest need.

Online PowerPoint training from Microsoft

If you use PowerPoint 2003 or 2007, Microsoft offers free training videos on their **office.microsoft.com** web site. In the Training section, select your version and you can see a list of available videos, usually running from 20-50 minutes in length. The videos focus on specific skills that you may want to learn and provide an overview that may be exactly what you need to get started using some of the features of the software.

Keynote online training from Apple

If you use Apple's keynote software, you can access video tutorials on Apple's web site at **www.apple.com/iwork**. In the Tutorials section, browse through the listed topics and view the videos that show you how to use the key features of the software.

PowerPoint newsgroup for questions

If you have a specific question on PowerPoint that you just can't figure out, tap in to the vast expertise available from the experts who regularly visit the PowerPoint newsgroup. Point your browser to

groups.google.com/group/microsoft.public.powerpoint and follow the instructions to search to see if your question has been asked and answered in the past (most of the common questions have been answered already). If you can't find an answer, post your question and within a few hours or days, someone will likely have posted the solution you are looking for.

Add-ins for PowerPoint

www.playsforcertain.com – play media clips properly every time.

www.pptools.com – Steve Rindsberg has a collection of add-ins that can help solve specific problems or speed up your presentation creation.

Bulk Book Orders

When you see the difference the KWICK method makes in the success of your presentations, you will want a copy for every member of your team. Discounts are offered when you order ten or more copies. Here is the discount schedule:

1-9 copies $29.95
10-25 copies $24.95
26 or more copies $19.95

(actual shipping cost will be added to your order total)

To place your bulk order, fill out the form below and fax it to (905) 826-2410 or call (905) 510-4911 to place your order by phone. Payment options include credit card, corporate or government purchase order or check. We will call to confirm payment method.

Name: _____

Company: _____

Address: _____

City: _____ State/Province: _____

Zip/Postal Code: _____

Telephone #: _____

Number of books to order: _____

Individual Book Order

You know how much the KWICK system has helped your presentations, why not order a copy as a gift for a colleague or friend. Fill out the form below and fax to (905) 826-2410 to order a copy today.

Name: _____

Address: _____

City: _____ State/Province: _____

Zip/Postal Code: _____

Telephone #: _____

Credit Card information (VISA or MasterCard only)

Card #: _____

Expiry Date: _____/_____   Security Code: _____

(the security code is found on the back of the card)

Cost of each book is $29.95 plus $3.50 for shipping and handling.

You can also order online at www.VisualSlideRevolution.com.

INDEX

S

Sales Presentation Slide
    Example, 26, 38, 47, 98,
    110, 123, 127
Scan a photo, 10, 79, 91
Screen capture, 24, 45, 93,
    94, 97
Share, 42
Slice, 42
Snapshot, 78, 97
Spreadsheet, 27, 32, 53
Steps in, 44
Story, 44, 79
Subordinate, 44
Sum of, 43
Survey results, 42

T

Table of, 45
T-chart, 76, 77
Testimonial, 45
Timeline, 44
Title, 35
Transparency, 70
Transparent, 61, 71, 92,
    105, 106, 109, 116, 117
Trend, 42

U

URL, 94

V

Venn diagram, 70
Video clip, 24, 45, 79, 84,
    85, 86

W

Web based presentation,
    120

When ... then, 45
WIMTT (What It Means To
    Them), 29
Words That Suggest The
    Visual, 24

CPSIA information can be obtained at www.ICGtesting.com
Printed in the USA
LVOW031159051111

253607LV00005B/9/P